PSYCHIC
COUNSELLING

Thorsons books by the same author:
Happy To Be Single
How To Stop Snoring

PSYCHIC COUNSELLING

Liz Hodgkinson

Aquarian/Thorsons
An Imprint of HarperCollins*Publishers*

Aquarian
An Imprint of HarperCollins*Publishers*
77–85 Fulham Palace Road
Hammersmith, London W6 8JB
1160 Battery Street
San Francisco, California 94111–1213

Published by Aquarian 1994

10 9 8 7 6 5 4 3 2 1

A catalogue record for this book
is available from the British Library

ISBN 1 85538 350 0

Printed in Great Britain by Mackays,
Chatham, Kent

CONTENTS

ACKNOWLEDGEMENTS

For expert help in preparing this book, the author would like to thank Brenda Marshall of the College of Psychic Studies; psychic counsellor Philippe Raynaud; Dr Lisa Sand, Inga Hooper, Mary Russell and Brenda Donald of Universitas Associates, and Betsey Longland.

INTRODUCTION

Many, if not most, intelligent people like to believe they are highly sceptical about psychic matters. They will tell you categorically that they don't believe in ghosts, spirits, the paranormal and all that kind of rubbish. Such people will also most probably fiercely maintain that all so-called 'psychics' and 'psychic counsellors'— mediums, astrologers, tarot readers and the like—are charlatans and quacks, people out to make easy money from the gullible by telling them that Auntie Mary in the spirit world is watching over them, or that they can see a large sum of money and a tall, dark, handsome stranger in the tea-leaves.

It may all sound on the face of it like so much nonsense, an insult to the intelligence of a sane, rational, logical person. I mean, how many of us have actually seen a ghost, heard voices in our ears or received guidance from an ancient Chinese, American Indian or Egyptian up there on the astral plane? Hardly any, outside the weird little world of mediums and psychics and spiritualists.

And yet none of us can ignore the fact that in our increasingly scientific and rational world, where every aspect of human behaviour has to be put under the microscope and subjected to double-blind clinical trials, where no phenomenon can be believed until it can be replicated in the laboratory, interest in psychic matters and psychic counselling and advice is growing at an astonishing rate. At one time confined to the end of the pier and party game seances in private houses, psychic counselling is now coming out into the open and being offered everywhere. Many large gyms, health clubs and health farms now have a psychic consultant along with their aerobics teachers, dieticians and trainers. If you look in almost any local paper, you will see an advertisement for psychic guidance. The 'stars', once confined to the seedier tabloid papers, are now found in many respectable, upmarket publications.

The British Royal Family—at least some of its younger members—and a growing number of business people, professional sportsmen and women and also politicians now regularly consult psychics. And I wouldn't mind betting that even the most scornful sceptic would at least be interested if they were offered a psychic reading or met a professional psychic by chance. There would be at least a *frisson* of fascination, a wondering whether this person really did have some kind of mysterious power—and what it might be.

Throughout the ages, in every single culture and tribe, there has been an awareness of the reality of the spirit world, of unseen forces which nevertheless have a significant influence on us all. In the earliest cultures, the greatest reality was felt to be that of the non-material. Buddhism tells us that all material things are an illusion, as they are impermanent and liable to decay, Hinduism emphasizes the indestructible nature of the individual human spirit throughout countless incarnations, and Judaism and Islam have very attractive heavens that the faithful and the saved go to after bodily death. Christianity is of course full of magic. It talks of the Father, Son and Holy Spirit—unseen, permanent, unchanging entities which nevertheless are extremely active, intervening intimately in the affairs of humankind.

In 1882, at the start of our present scientific age, The Society for Psychical Research was formed in Britain to try and make sense of the psychic phenomena which suddenly seemed to be manifesting everywhere, by subjecting them to rigorous scientific trials. Spiritualism had already taken hold on both sides of the Atlantic and an ever-growing number of people were contacting, or alleging to contact, discarnate entities.

Stories of levitation, of spewing out ectoplasm, of conjuring up the spirits of long-dead people, of predicting dire events, were getting into the newspapers. The new profession of 'medium'— the only one at the time to have more women than men—was becoming extremely popular, and some mediums were claiming astonishing powers. It was time, decided a group of well-heeled, leisured Cambridge scientists, to put all these claims to the test, and try to establish once and for all whether there were such things as ghosts and spirits and poltergeists, whether clairvoyance, otherwise known as the 'sixth sense' was a reality, and whether reports of *déjà vu* and telepathy had any substance.

Since then, scientific investigations—undertaken mainly by male academics and psychologists—have proceeded apace and are still going on. At the headquarters of the SPR any member of the public can get permission to look at the painstaking work that has been undertaken, read about the often years-long ghost-hunting exercises and the ingenious experiments that have been designed scientifically to test telepathy or other mysterious powers.

These show that although very many mediums and psychics have unceremoniously been exposed as fakes, there is also a large body of research which indicates that there actually is something else at work, something which cannot entirely be explained by disturbed brain patterns, mental illness, hallucinations or wishful thinking. It is that 'something' which I shall be talking about in this book. My own investigations and research have shown me beyond all possible doubt that what we call the paranormal is a reality and that some people— perhaps all of us to some extent—possess talents and gifts which can loosely be labelled 'psychic'.

In its simplest terms, to be psychic is to have the ability to receive information through sources other than the five sensory organs. I believe that the 'sixth sense' is as tangible in its way as a gift for painting, music or making money. I believe that some people do hear voices, see entities that the rest of us don't see, and gain an inkling of events to come which evades standard economists and futurologists.

I also believe that, at its best, psychic counselling can help where other kinds of therapy and counselling might fail. So the main purpose of this book is to describe, as clearly as possible, what is meant by psychic counselling, and why you may want to consider this form of help.

One of the main advantages of psychic counselling, when it works, is that it is extremely quick. For whereas standard psychotherapy and psychoanalysis can take months or even years, psychic counselling can often achieve astonishing results in a matter of hours. This is because psychic counsellors make full use of an ancient ability often derided or marginalized in our supposedly rational and logical world—that of intuition. Without always knowing exactly how or why, the truth of a situation flashes into their mind. The best counsellors can spend a few minutes looking at you and then 'see' your past, present and aspects of your future in a kind of vision.

But although the best psychics can be wonderful, there is of course a lot of scope for trickery, for sheer bad advice and for leading people up the garden path. So what should you expect from a psychic? Is there any kind of quality control in this fast-growing world, and how do you know whether you have booked up a reading with somebody genuine or not? These are important questions that this book sets out to answer. Because I myself have greatly benefited from psychic counselling, and am still benefiting, I feel I want to pass on what I have learned. I must also, however, say that I have been on the receiving end of psychic counselling or advice which has done me no good at all, which has made me afraid, and which has had nothing but a negative influence.

So how can you evaluate the quality of the counselling? Because the psychic gift is so little understood, it can be difficult to find a means of appraising the worth of any particular reading or counselling session. If you wanted to be a doctor or a dentist, you would have to go through a recognized course of training and then be subject to a rigorous code of professional conduct. You would not be allowed to kill patients at random, to tell them you were in love with them or suggest that you performed all kinds of experimental procedures on them. Any doctor or dentist who behaved like this would soon be struck off and not allowed to practise ever again. There are no such strictures with psychic counselling. Anybody at all— whether possessing psychic abilities or not—can call themselves a psychic counsellor and quite legally set up in business. Once in business, such people can perform any acts they can get away with. They can tell their patients that the way to overcome their problems is to go to bed with them, they can ask you to hand over large sums of money so that the spirits can come through, they can advise you to engage in illegal acts, encourage you to take mind-altering drugs or embezzle funds from your place of work. I'm not saying that the majority of counsellors will behave like this, or even that this kind of behaviour is at all common. The point I'm making is that they *could* carry on like this, and so long as nobody complained, there would be nothing to stop them. Because there is no formally recognized training for psychic counsellors, because there is no professional body monitoring conduct, the whole field remains a free for all, and one that anybody at all can enter.

One of the reason for this is that, until recently at least, psychic counselling has been considered relatively harmless, a self-indulgent game that amuses some people but which really is of very little importance. I, though, along with a growing number of people who have seriously considered the field, believe that psychic counsellors and consultants have the capacity to do people at least as much good—or harm—as doctors or dentists, or members of any other profession. Perhaps they have a greater capacity, because they are tuning into our deepest wishes, fears and hopes.

Fortunately, my own experience and research has shown me that most people calling themselves psychic counsellors are not wicked Rasputins or evil people trying to put 'the fluence' on you for their own dastardly purposes. At the same time, though, it is important to be very careful, simply because although most are undoubtedly well-meaning, they may not have had any real training either in counselling techniques or psychic development. They are, often, simply people who have acknowledged or discovered in themselves a psychic gift of some kind and have decided to utilize it.

Also, it is an unfortunate fact that many people now setting up as psychic counsellors are those who have signally failed in other fields of endeavour. They may be people who have failed to hold down other jobs, who have never been able to pass exams for a proper profession, and have decided to do this work after coming to the end of every other line.

At the other end of the scale are people who take their work completely seriously, who have a genuine desire to serve humanity, and whose counselling and guidance is of the highest order.

With something so mysterious as the paranormal, however is one to tell the difference?

I hope that this book will bridge the gap, and provide a sensible way in to this world which is still hedged around with so much mystery, superstition and fear. Most of the current books on psychic matters seem to fall into two distinct categories. One the one hand there are the earnest ghost-hunting books, which are full of detailed and careful experiments, and which go out of their way to be rational and scientific. Most of these books are written by male academics who have an abiding interest in trying to pin down or explain unusual or anomalous phenomena. Such books tend to be deadly dull and of interest only to the serious psychic researcher. The other main type of book is that written by a practising psychic or medium, usually a woman, which is full of unproven assertions about spirits, astral planes, ethereal bodies, chakras, auras and discarnate entities. Although these books are usually very readable and are full of warm and inspiring human stories, they would do little to convince a sceptic that there was any sense at all in what was being said.

In fact, there are now several people who are setting out to prove conclusively that there are no such things as mysterious powers and that all people calling themselves psychics or mediums are just very clever operators, wangling questions so that the answers look like astonishing insights. The most famous psychic investigator is American magician James Randi, who 'exposed' a whole series of mediums, clairvoyants and astrologers on a six-part series on British television.

For his programme, Randi gathered together crystal healers, astrologers, dowsers, metal-benders and others professing paranormal abilities and asked them to take part in laboratory-type experiments to show whether they really were exhibiting any kind of extra-sensory perception. It must be said that most of the mediums and psychics on the programme made a very poor showing, thus appearing to back up Randi's claims that there was nothing at all mysterious or beyond chance in what they were divining or predicting. However, it should be noted that Randi's method of interviewing and editing of the pro-grammes meant that he could avoid showing any successes achieved by the psychics.

Practising psychics have answered critics like Randi by saying that their powers come and go, that they are never strong in the presence of a sceptic and that they cannot always perform to order. James Randi is convinced they are all pulling the wool over their own and other people's eyes, and trying to make themselves seem special by alleging unusual powers or perceptions, or making out they have been chosen to be the recipients of divine wisdom from the astral sphere, wisdom that is withheld from the rest of us, and has to be laboriously 'channelled' by these special people.

In America now there is a huge body of 'channelled' literature purporting to come from ancient entities existing on the ethereal plane. Few rationally-minded people take it seriously—most, like James Randi, just laugh at it or try to dismiss it as so much delusion and self-deception. Some, perhaps much of it, may be. But I also feel the time has come for those of us who do see ourselves as rational, sane, logical, not easily taken in, to take on board the reality of the psychic world and understand it for what it is. It is time, I believe, for us to harness it for our own self-enlightenment and to help and guide us at difficult times of our lives. When a genuine psychic gift is allied to a love of humanity, a wish to serve and help, then it can be of inestimable value for those in need of healing, nurturing and comfort.

The trouble is, the psychic gift is not only given to those motivated to help their fellows. It is, like any other talent, neutral in itself, and can be used for good or ill. Just as great painters and musicians do not always have impeccable characters and can lie, steal and cheat, so can those possessing psychic abilities. So anybody offering psychic guidance and advice should be a serious, responsible person. The guidance received should be of an order that you could not easily get anywhere else, such as from talking to a friend, or going to see a counsellor at your local doctor's surgery. Because genuinely gifted psychic counsellors are able to tap the deepest recesses of their clients' emotions, there should be no party game element about it, no feeling that you are there just for fun, to see what happens.

Why do people consult psychic counsellors, in fact? In a world which is changing ever more rapidly, where there seem to be no certainties, and where religion has signally failed to offer any genuine help, it is perhaps hardly surprising that ever more people—even on occasions the highly sceptical—turn to the psychic world for help. When our feelings overwhelm us, when we feel we just can't cope, we are liable to seek help from a source which, at times when we feel supremely comfortable, we may have dismissed as ridiculous.

I'm thinking here specifically of bereavement. Very many people have become interested in psychic matters when they have suffered a terrible or sudden loss, a devastation with which they simply cannot come to terms. Very frequently, this will be the untimely death of a beloved child or partner. Because the premature death seems so unfair, so lacking in any proper explanation or reason, the bereaved person will try to get some comfort from somewhere. At such times, it may seem rational, rather than irrational, to try to get in touch once again

with the person who has just died, to maintain contact, to be
reassured that they still exist somewhere, so great is the wish to
believe they are not just gone for ever, or that their truncated
lives were not in vain.

Perhaps bereavement provides the greatest single motivation
for getting in touch with a psychic, but life doesn't have to
have dealt you a terrible blow for you to take advantage of this
kind of help. You might be at a crossroads in your life and want
some clarification of the right path to take, you might be
hearing voices and wondering whether you are schizophrenic
or otherwise mentally deranged, or you might want to know
whether a particular person, job or house move is right for
you. Whatever your reason for wanting to see a psychic
counsellor, it should be serious and not frivolous. There can be
no guarantee, of course, that any individual counsellor will be
able to provide you with the answers or help to put you on the
accurate path. But what they will be able to do, if they are
genuine, is to help you sort out what you really want. They
will not advise you on a particular route, but will help you to
see the pros and cons of whatever choices you might make,
and enable you to see patterns where you may only have seen
random, chaotic events.

A good, but simple example of accurate psychic counselling
is something that happened to me not long ago. I had bought a
very expensive flat which I had decorated lavishly. After a
couple of years, during which time mortgage repayments
soared and my income plummeted, I thought I would have to
move. I could see no possible way of affording to stay in the
flat, and there appeared to be no easy solution to my problem.

A couple of women I knew with profound psychic powers
came to see me when I was at a very low ebb and panicking
wildly about what to do. They sat in my living-room while I
asked them if they had any ideas on what I should do. After a
few minutes, one of them spoke.

She said, 'I can see your difficulties. But you have worked
hard to make this flat absolutely beautiful and you have to
remember that moving house is a very traumatic experience.'

That was all—but it was all I needed. Those positive words gave me the strength and confidence to try and stay in the flat. As things turned out, it was the best decision. In despair, I had been about to put my flat on the market at a time when house prices were going down daily. But then my panic receded, bank interest levels went down and my income went back up. The psychics could probably see what I, in my panic-ridden state, was unable to. But—and this is vitally important—they did not attempt to tell me what to do.

Being open-minded about psychic counselling can, as I've discovered for myself, open up a window on a whole new exciting world and bring into being a far more positive way of looking at things. It can enable us to fit in pieces of the jigsaw, to view our lives as a harmonious whole rather than a series of unrelated and random events. It can help us to have a more charitable view of our fellow humans, our relatives, partners, employers and children. It can help us to feel connected, rather than separated. It can help us to take charge of our lives rather than have the feeling that we are victims, caught up in a capricious chain of events way beyond our control or input. It can make us feel more confident and serene.

Even if none of us can prove to professional sceptics like James Randi that the paranormal is, or can be, a reality, we can know that the proof of the pudding is in the eating. We can come to believe in the reality of our own feelings, and not imagine that reason and logic are superior to emotion and gut reaction.

But because any form of intuitive counselling has to be tempered by reason and logic, we should all take on board the fact that common sense plays a large part as well. While admitting that there may be another kind of reality, we should also make sure our feet stay firmly on the ground and remember to put all 'psychic' matters and experiences through the hopper of our intellect. A good experience of psychic counselling should enable us to expand our consciousness and not shut down our reasoning powers.

Psychic counsellors can definitely help us—but we have to

be careful. They can vary as much as garages, restaurants, hotels or anything else in life. And, as with most professions, there are a few supremely good counsellors, a whole host of mediocre ones and a very few downright bad or criminal ones.

My hope is that this book will help and enlighten all those who have ever been intrigued by the idea of psychic counselling, but might have hesitated to try it for themselves, to gain the very best that is available from this rapidly-expanding field.

ONE

EXPLAINING THE UNEXPLAINED

Extra-sensory perception is a continuing mystery, a classic case of 'the unexplained'. If somebody had genuinely succeeded in explaining it, then of course, it would no longer be unexplained, but crystal clear! The most I can hope to do is to say how it appears to me in the light of the latest research, and give my own observations and experience. For this book, I shall not attempt to try and determine whether there are such things as ghosts or poltergeists, or whether ectoplasm really can come out of the mouths of mediums. I shall, though, before we get on to the practicalities of psychic counselling, try to explain what I understand by psychic phenomena as far as is relevant to this book—that is, the explanations which seem to make most sense and which may help to bring about some understanding of psychic counselling.

In past ages, most people were content to believe in things unseen, in spirits, demons, fairies and powers beyond the grave, even if they never experienced any of these for themselves. Such things did not need 'explaining' because they were so self-evident. It was obvious to most early cultures that there were spirits, and abundantly clear that the material body and visible reality were not all there was. If they were, life made no kind of sense, for what propelled it, what animated it?

Over the past hundred years or so, at least in the West, there have been strenuous attempts to try and come to terms with the paranormal. Even the most sceptical researcher has realized that it is impossible to ignore it altogether. There have been enough allegations of seeing ghosts, of hearing voices, of communicating with the dead, for the subject at least to merit investigation, even if a large number of the allegations have turned out to be fraudulent or impossible to prove. Even if none of them whatever were to be proved beyond all possible doubt, this would still leave the inescapable fact that large numbers of people, for some reason, *need* to believe in things unseen and unheard by our sense organs.

Most psychical researchers have found, to their cost, that when they exposed a fraudulent medium, or showed that alleged poltergeist activity was simply children mucking about, most people just went on believing regardless. They still flocked to see the fraudulent mediums, still felt the poltergeist activity was genuine. We *want* to believe that some people have special powers, that there is more to heaven and earth than simply molecules and chemicals interacting with each other. Not even the most fervent humanists, atheists and rationalists have managed to stamp out this belief. Nor have they yet proved that there is nothing in the paranormal, that there are no such things as unusual powers. In fact, the more that psychologists, geneticists and researchers probe, the more unexplained phenomena we seem to be left with.

One might imagine that 100 years of serious scientific research into the paranormal would have discovered one of two things: either that it was all delusion and fantasy, or that there were definitely unseen forces at work. In fact, hard evidence is as inconclusive as ever.

What the research so far has shown, to all those who have even a glimmer of an open mind about the subject, is that there are, indeed, happenings, events and perceptions which cannot easily be explained by known scientific laws. But it seems we need science, or scientific instruments, to show us more than this, to show us that strange phenomena are *real*, at least in some sense, even if we cannot formulate any laws by which they might happen.

Sensitive instruments have now enabled scientists to monitor human brain waves and to compare the brain wave of a psychic with that of an ordinary person. The measurements show that when a psychic is operating, their brain waves are far slower and deeper, more like those that occur in sleep, than those of an ordinary person. It has also been shown that a psychic's brain waves can affect those of the client, enabling them to slow down to a point where perception is altered.

This ability to affect the brain waves of another person has been called 'the relaxation response', and it has been shown that this is where healing happens. There appears to be some potent transfer of energy from the psychic to the client, but what that energy is, where it comes from and just what its purpose is have not yet been defined.

Laboratory experiments have also established that some people professing psychic powers can alter the growth rate of plants and can send out thoughts that are picked up almost simultaneously by people the other side of the globe. The psychic powers of animals have been well documented, and there is some evidence to show that small children are psychic, in that they can makes guesses way beyond chance.

The psychic powers of children seem to disappear at about the age of seven, the well-known 'age of reason', and from that age, most children just forget that they ever had premonitions, could guess cards accurately on the other side of a screen or had imaginary playmates. They become 'normal'—or at least their perception of extra-sensory matters dims.

In some cases, however, the powers seem to be retained into adulthood. At one level, psychics are people who seem to have extra perception, an extra sensitivity to people, places, events, atmospheres, and it is this which marks them out from the rest of us. Indeed, in some circles, psychics are known as 'sensitives'. Some psychics have realized their gift and are utilizing it, while others remain unaware, and find their lives extremely confusing as a result.

There seems little doubt that some people do hear voices and see apparitions which for most of us are invisible, and that these visions are as real to them as images on a television or cinema screen are to the rest of us. At the same time, most psychics—at least when they are adult—are aware that most people do not see what they see.

One example of this is auras. Many psychic children see coloured auras around people and their earliest paintings depict this. They are then told by adults that people are not surrounded by colours of the rainbow—because the adults can't see anything like this—and so they learn to stop representing them. But they continue to see these coloured lights—and learn to keep this ability quiet until they are adult, when they may use this to help and heal people. Or, they may just remain confused by this strange ability which seems to have no useful function whatever.

But what is the nature of this extra sensitivity, and why do some people possess it while others don't? It seems likely that those possessed of psychic gifts are able to tap into a source of extra energy which feeds them with information and gives them increased awareness.

In most early societies, those with extra sensitivity and awareness were honoured and revered. At the very least, such people were feared and held in awe. Sometimes, they were burned at the stake for heresy, simply because they saw things too clearly, things which were not apparent to others. But whatever the outcome, the idea that certain people possessed mysterious powers was not in question. During the terrible witch hunts in the sixteenth and seventeenth centuries, clever, educated men sincerely believed that harmless old women were in league with the devil. They genuinely thought that by burning witches at the stake, they were casting out evil. And although most of those burned at the stake were women, the fire was not reserved for the female sex. Men who were considered to have evil powers were also liable to be burned to death. So although psychics and seers have always been considered in some way special, in many ages their gift of special sight or special perception has been as much a burden as a blessing.

One of the curses of the psychic or the seer has always been that their prophecies and predictions have not been not believed. The prophecies of Cassandra, in ancient Greece, were never believed, and the soothsayer who told Caesar to beware the Ides of March was dismissed as a dreamer. The witches in Shakespeare's play *Macbeth* foretold what would happen, and Macbeth vainly tried to subvert the prophecy. Poets, painters and creative people have always known that there are those who have powers of insight denied the general masses, but also that there is often a high price to pay for that clairvoyance.

Our own age is no different. Although we like to dismiss those who seem to have the gift of prophecy, we still feel uncomfortable and suspicious of them. There is a wish to exclude them, to banish them to the sidelines, to refuse to take what they say seriously.

One of the reasons for this might be that the psychic gift has always been seen as something allied to the feminine, something receptive and passive, rather than active and aggressive. Mediums go into a trance while the spirits talk, they pick up energies from other people or other sources and they have to go into a meditative or relaxed state in order to work at all. All this is far removed from the active male principle which is so revered in our society, far removed from the scientific way of doing things, in which active experiments have to be set up and results quantified and analysed. The psychic gift, whatever it might ultimately be, is something soft and flowing, something which does not seek to impose itself in any way on others. It is there if it is required, if not, it may just vanish unappreciated.

Ultimately, to be psychic means to hear that voice—or those voices—inside, to trust them, and not have to try to explain everything by reason and logic. Psychic people know that some things, such as falling in love, having premonitions about people or events, or picking up atmospheres, cannot be simply or easily explained, but are realities which dramatically affect our behaviour. Even the most logical, rational, unemotional person can fall in love, for example—and have no idea what is happening. But the feelings are real enough.

For psychics, the ultimate reality is a *feeling* reality rather than a *thinking* reality. Although reason and logic should not fly out of the window, they come in later, not initially, to explain what may be happening.

Some people have said that trying to explain the unexplained is like trying to get a four year old child to understand
the theory of relativity—an impossible task. But because we
want to understand, we need to understand, we have at least
to try to explain it in ways that won't be insulting to people's
intelligence.

It certainly seems true that we do not understand how the
universe works, we do not understand exactly what creates
life, and we do not understand the exact mechanisms by which
plants, animals and humans may communicate with each other
on subtle levels, other than by verbal, visual or auditory
means. We do know, however, that there are extremely
complicated means of communication and gaining information
in existence, and it seems fair to say that psychic matters
constitute the most complicated type of communication of all.

Some psychics believe they are in touch with discarnate
entities. This may take the form of hearing disembodied voices,
or it may be that one particular entity chooses to attach itself to
somebody and has a name and a lineage. British medium Ivy
Northage has for years worked through the Chinese entity
Chan, for example, and spiritual healer George Chapman
performs his spirit operations through the guidance of long-
dead surgeon Dr Lang, a real person who died in the 1930s.

But not all psychics feel they are in touch with disembodied
spirits from other planes of existence. Some define the voices
they hear as coming from their own higher selves, while others
say they are tapping into the universal unconscious, or the
Akashic records, an astral 'log book' which supposedly contains
all the information about every human being who has ever
lived.

How does this relate to psychic counselling? It seems to me
that in this area the 'unexplained' falls into several categories:
intuition, telepathy, clairvoyance and mediumship. As intuition
seems perhaps the easiest (and the least weird) of these, I will
deal with it first.

INTUITION

All of us on occasion use our intuition, or gut feelings, whether or not we realize it, but psychics have learned to *trust* this faculty. When tuning into their clients, they will hardly ever use the rational, logical approach, but will rely on this other means to yield valuable information and insights.

A good psychic counsellor does not need to know who you are, what your name is or even why you have come. They should be able to 'divine' why you have come, by picking up signals, of distress, discomfort or curiosity which you have given. They will be able to tune into your vibrations. Why?

Because, if they have a genuine gift, they will not be using their own ego, but will be able to concentrate fully on you. It is partly this power of concentration which will enable them to tell you things which seem astonishing, which makes it possible for them to read you like a book. One mistake that people often make about intuition is that it is just there and can be tapped into. In fact, like any other activity, intuition needs to be nurtured and brought out with quite deliberate practice. One faculty which has to be consciously developed, in order to maximize intuitive powers, is that of concentration. For instance, a good psychic will be concentrating entirely on you and be undistracted by any other happening.

Contrast this with going to the doctor's surgery, for instance, where the doctor may be interrupted by the receptionist, by phone calls, by their own thoughts. One reason that doctors' diagnoses are so often false or partial is because very few doctors ever give you their full attention, and almost none have been taught to use or trust their intuition. In fact, intuition is a faculty that is stamped out of most doctors by their training.

Another major difference between a standard psychiatrist or psychotherapist and a psychic counsellor is that the psychiatrist will be using large amounts of book knowledge to try and get at the root of their patients' problems. By contrast, a psychic will 'feel' things about people—there are no standard textbooks on psychic counselling, so there can be no reliance on this source of information. All has to come from the client, and of course, from the experience the counsellor may have built up over the years.

This approach enables psychic counsellors to treat all their clients as individuals, rather than people who behave as they do because they were abused as children, or because they were bottle-fed or adopted as children. Because a psychic relies on their intuition, they will have no preconceptions about the people who come to see them. They will know that some people are strengthened by an unhappy childhood while others may be made weak and vulnerable.

As children, we all have strong intuitive powers. We can deduce things not by logic and reason, because we have not developed these faculties, but by somehow 'knowing' the answer.

When I was a child of five, I was aware that there was something 'different' about a man who worked with my mother. For some reason, I felt highly suspicious of him, and became tongue-tied and awkward in his presence. It wasn't until many years later I learned that he and my mother were deeply in love. At the time, of course, I knew nothing of love and sex, but I somehow knew that this man took me away from my mother, from her full attention, that he was somehow a threat.

Practising psychics have to bring this hidden faculty to the fore to be able to help their clients. They have to become, in some ways, like children. This is one reason why they are often considered to be rather 'simple'.

Whether we consider ourselves psychic or not, we all know for a certainty when we feel happy or miserable, depressed, enthusiastic, ecstatic or devastated. We also know how we feel about people—some of them we like, others we dislike; some we strongly like or dislike, and a few we may loathe or hate. With some people, we feel a strong rapport, often known as 'chemistry', although nobody has ever described exactly which chemicals are involved in a strong liking or love for a particular person. When we go into a room, we immediately pick up an atmosphere—perhaps of peace and harmony, perhaps of discord and hate. These feelings are completely real to us, even though we may hesitate to describe exactly why we feel as we do. We all pick up atmospheres, we all feel fear, even when there is no need to.

So, at its simplest level, intuition can be described as a survival instinct. Animals instinctively know who is kind to them, who feels fear, who feels love, and because they have no speech or powers of deduction, they act accordingly. And in humans, intuition comes very much come to the fore at times when we are nervous or unsure of ourselves.

When we go for a job interview, for example, we may instantly get strong feelings about whether we would like this job, whether we could see ourselves working in such an environment, whether we could get on with the person who would be our boss. All these impressions crowd together in an instant and, at the same time, the interviewer is getting similar impressions about us. But all too often, when interviewers look at a CV, they take more notice of it than of gut reactions. An impressive set of qualifications can override the initial impression, for good or ill.

Similarly, we on the receiving end might not quite like the feel of the building or the impression given by the interviewer, but if it's a better job, a step up the ladder, with more money and better prospects than our previous one, we may override our intuition and take the job if offered, even if it doesn't 'feel' right. Such a job will never, though, work out. Whenever we don't go with our gut feelings, disaster follows.

The same thing happens in relationships. Very many men and women have in their minds a blueprint of the kind of person they'd like to marry or set up home with and then seek out that person in a coldly logical way. Psychologist Heather Formaini has drawn attention to the fact that very many men get to their thirties and then think, 'Hey, it's about time I got married, set up home, settled down' and so on. They then look for a suitable 'victim', somebody who more or less fits the bill, and imagine that side of their lives is taken care of forever. Politicians particularly fall into this trap, which is why so many of them come spectacular croppers when they are caught having affairs with much younger or more attractive or livelier women: they have sat on their feelings and obeyed the dictates of reason and logic, but discover that their feelings find a way to come to the surface after all and put all their careful control in jeopardy.

So intuition is a very useful commodity, but how do we explain it? There are no replicable laboratory experiments which can show us how it works. All we know is that it does. Also that it seems to work best during periods of relaxation and meditation. When our minds are quiet, they go into alpha mode, the level of creativity and calm, generating slower brain waves. Then the right answers often come to us. (During alert, conscious hours, we usually function on the faster beta frequency.)

If answers come with startling clarity, we should not ignore them but go with them. A few years ago, when still living with my husband, I had the overriding feeling that I must leave him and branch out on a new life on my own. It wasn't that I hated him, more that I felt that period of my life had come to an end and it was time to move on to something new. The feeling grew so strong that eventually it could not be contained, even though 'logically' it did not seem to make sense. We had fairly recently bought an old house we were still in the process of doing up, and if I left him I would at best have only half the money to buy a new house and set myself up. I would be poorer and life would be more difficult. Yet, it had to happen. And as soon as I had made up my mind that this was something I must do, then the way was made clear for me to do it.

The difference between 'ordinary' people and practising psychics, though, is that the psychics get these feelings all the time, and not just about their own lives, but about other people's. They get flashes of inspiration about what others should do, a path that is closed to most of us, as we do not take enough interest in the lives of others. We might get occasional flashes of intuition in relation to our own lives, but psychics get them about all sorts of things. They may get 'feelings' about what will happen in politics, in the economy and about the clients who sit in front of them. By going into alpha mode, which they can do at will—or which they learn to do on psychic unfoldment courses—they can plug into another person's subconscious.

Psychics have no doubt about the strength and accuracy of these feelings, and some have described sittings with clients as bringing out information which the client already knows, but which has been buried deep in the subconscious. Intuition may be described a method of bringing to conscious awareness information the unconscious mind already knows, a way of bridging the gap between the two. The less intuitive we are, the greater the gap, the more intuitive, the narrower the gap.

Although psychics vary greatly from each other in their powers, their wisdom, their insights, they have one thing in common—they are all people who continue to trust their intuition, their gut feelings. They are people who will look you straight in the eye and say they don't know why, but they get this feeling that you will soon be moving house, emigrating to Australia or whatever, even though nothing like this is indicated in your present circumstances.

In later chapters I'll be talking about how you as a client can most usefully respond to a psychic's intuition about you, as it may not always be 100 per cent accurate.

TELEPATHY

With telepathy, we start to get into more obviously 'psychic' areas. The word 'telepathy' simply means the ability to communicate thoughts and ideas soundlessly, wordlessly, from one person to another. Most of us have daily experience of telepathy in relation to things and people we know well. We may think of somebody for no apparent reason and then we receive a letter from them or they ring us up. Very often, when I am working, I suddenly think of somebody whom I haven't seen or spoken to for months, maybe years. When this happens, I can almost always guarantee that somehow that person will become significant in my life. Perhaps they won't be all that significant, but they will play an important part for a bit.

Similarly, we all experience telepathic contact, if only fleetingly, with people we know well or love very much. The difference between us and practising psychics is that the psychics may experience telepathic communication in relation to people, places and things they may hardly know at all.

The brain waves that we spoke about in relation to intuition have also been studied in attempts to define and pin down telepathy. There is some evidence to suggest that telepathic transmission happens most effectively when the brain is functioning on the alpha frequency, a mode, as we have seen, that psychics can go into much more easily than most of us.

Although telepathy, and telepathic powers, are generally considered something highly desirable, most of us should be happy that we are not receiving telepathic signals all the time. If we were, we would be picking up things from other people constantly and might have difficulty in distinguishing their thoughts from our own. That is often what happens with psychics, especially untrained ones—they cannot always distinguish between their own thoughts and those of other people. They are also so very sensitive to impressions and communications at levels below the conscious that they are open to all kinds of impressions which can make life extremely disturbing.

People often imagine that if somebody is reading their thoughts, or trying to, that this person is somehow trying to gain power over them. But, as with intuition, telepathy is a faculty which can be developed fully only when there is no ego at work and when one person is not trying to influence another or affect their thoughts in any way.

Many people have used a telepathic gift, or apparent gift, to 'divine' what people's names are or what card they are holding in their hand. In stage shows this is almost always achieved through sleight of hand or trickery rather than actual telepathic powers. For this reason, and because it is so very easy to pull the wool over people's eyes, as James Randi has shown with his clever magician's tricks on stage, telepathy has received rather a bad name and a bad image.

It seems to me that there is nothing all that mysterious about telepathy or about using this ability in everyday life. All it really comes down to is having the knack of tapping into somebody else's subconscious and being able to bring these thoughts to some kind of conscious expression. But, of course, we are all wary—and rightly so—of those people who seem able to read us like a book, to know more about us than we know ourselves.

Yet all of us, whether we realize it or not, are sending out subconscious signals all the time. We do this by our body language, our dress, our speech, our accent, our mannerisms. It is not possible to hide very much from a truly perceptive person. But most of us are so concerned with ourselves, so concerned with what other people might think about us, we are so lacking in confidence and so full of fears, that we do not pick up these signals as much from other people as we would if our minds were not filled with so many negative and fearful thoughts.

The difference between us and psychics who take their work seriously is that psychics make conscious efforts to clear their minds from garbage in order to amplify their telepathic abilities. They allow themselves to 'connect' more to other people, but at the same time develop the ability to 'shut down' so that impressions don't crowd in when they are not wanted.

CLAIRVOYANCE

This faculty is intimately associated with being psychic and means, literally, 'clear seeing.' In some instances, it is taken to mean an ability to see into the future.

In common with intuition and telepathy, clairvoyance is an ability we all have to some extent—it's just that psychics have a more developed faculty than most of us. They can, in some way that seems hidden from the rest of us, 'see' or visualize what is going to happen, or what might already be happening.

Again, this ability may be less mysterious than at first appears. Although we may not understand the exact mechanism by which clairvoyance works, we know that full use of the intuitive faculty enables deductions and inferences to be made about present circumstances which may be inaccessible to reason and logic. We know that economists and futurologists almost always get things wrong when talking about what will happen in the economy. This is because they are working with very blinkered vision and do not take emotions and the effects of certain actions on board. For example, ever since I was a young adult, galloping inflation and easy mortgages in Britain ensured that most of us who bought houses and got onto the property spiral would soon make a nice profit when we sold our houses. It seemed to us in our bones that this could not go on for ever, but because it all seemed to be working so well, we fell for it and kept on falling for it, fixing up ever higher mortgages and living in ever more expensive houses, something our parents and grandparents had never done. On the back of this house boom, estate agents grew rich and proliferated, as did lawyers, as ever more people moved on to a bigger and better house every few years. Politicians and right-wing economists assured us that we were now all rich, we were now all house-owners and we had never had it so good.

A clairvoyant, though, would have seen that no ultimate good could come of it, because our actions were disobeying universal laws. We were encouraged to be greedy, to borrow vast sums of money we could not pay back for many, many years and to live on credit—a never-never land that was bound to catch up with us. When the property boom collapsed, thousands of people were left stranded, having bought a dream which went sour, which was bound to go sour, as it could not possibly go on for ever.

A genuine clairvoyant understands that there are implacable universal laws which we break at our peril. This is knowledge and understanding which we could all have, if we chose to access it. Most of us don't, though, because we find it uncomfortable. And clairvoyants often find life uncomfortable too, when nobody will listen to them.

During the height of the property boom, for example, who would have wanted to be told that we should always live within our means and not borrow enormous sums of money that we could not hope to pay back? Who would have listened to those who issued dire warnings that it was actually wrong to borrow these large sums, that somebody would have to pay and account for it in the end? No, we preferred to go on living in a fool's paradise, and were all very shocked when the free and easy credit-living days came to an end.

It's the same story with the environment, with pollution and with any form of shallow hedonism. Clairvoyants know that every action has a consequence and that whatever you do eventually rebounds back on you. Unless you live in harmony with your own nature and with resources, all satisfaction will be short-lived. The reason clairvoyants can see into the future is because they apply these laws.

Clairvoyance is often seen as a wholly mysterious activity, because so many people professing this ability use objects such as crystal balls or want to hold something of yours, such as a wedding ring, in their hands while they foretell your future. In fact, there is nothing particularly mysterious about the objects they may use. They merely act as amplifiers, something to concentrate on which will facilitate the ability to see more clearly what is happening.

The clairvoyant ability is highly variable. No clairvoyant is accurate all the time and any person using ESP is liable to pick up wrong information. This is why anything which is told you by a clairvoyant should be carefully assessed in the light of logic and reason. None of the deductive faculties should be suspended, but they should come even more into play during any display of apparent clairvoyance.

Because people are so interested in clairvoyance, and because it seems so mysterious and peculiar, clairvoyants themselves are often liable to make out their gift is greater than it is. Nobody has the gift of clear-seeing all the time, and in many cases, psychics can be hopelessly wrong. The gift of clear sight comes from innate ability which is then practised and honed, like any other native talent. It comes from getting rid of your own negative tendencies, particularly the ego, as with intuition and telepathy, and being able to view other people non-judgementally and without relation to yourself. On the whole, the more you see people as aspects or extensions of yourself, the less will be your own clairvoyance. The more you are able to detach, and see yourself and everybody else as actors on a vast stage, playing out your parts, the more these abilities will come to the fore, and the more you can rely on them.

Over the years, many scientists and engineers have devised complicated and ingenious experiments to test clairvoyance and other forms of ESP. One of the foremost researchers in this area is Arthur Ellison, for many years Professor of Electrical and Electronic Engineering at the City University, London. These are not perhaps areas usually very closely associated with psychic matters, but Professor Ellison, who is also a Vice-President of the British Society for Psychical Research, has long believed that the paranormal is an absolute reality, perhaps the only absolute reality, and has spent a lifetime trying to prove it. He believes the main difference between clairvoyance and telepathy is that with clairvoyance, something is 'seen' directly, whereas with telepathy the information is obtained from somebody else's mind already containing this information.

Is this clear? The distinction becomes apparent with simple

card-guessing games. If somebody holds a card, and you divine what it is, you are using telepathy. In other words, the other person knows what the card is, and you are reading what is in their minds. With clairvoyance, by contrast, you can look at a card face down and 'see' what it is.

I must say, though, that card-guessing games are, in my experience, not a good test of either. My ex-husband learned a highly complicated card game with which for very many years he fooled everybody into believing he was telepathic. In common with professional showmen, he used a crystal ball and much mumbo-jumbo to make the trick seem more mysterious, and not even the most rational, sceptical and sophisticated person ever guessed that it was a trick. All thought that somehow he was tapping into their minds, although he wasn't at all. He actually knew, by completely non-telepathic means, which card was being held. Only I ever guessed that it was a trick, and that was because I couldn't possibly work it out. The fact that I couldn't work it out meant that I knew it was a trick. My lack of mathematical ability helped me here. For all I knew, when I was at school, other pupils got maths answers right by telepathy. There seemed no way to me that it was possible to get them right, and the whole process was, and remains, beyond me (and many others).

I think in some ways that those of us who are not scientifically minded, who find it difficult to grasp simple laws of physics, maths and chemistry, are *less* likely to be taken in by apparent displays of telepathy and clairvoyance which do not obey known laws than those with a scientific background.

Professor Ellison has set up very many experiments whereby subjects, both ordinary people and known psychics, have been asked to divine information by pressing numbers on specially designed electrical boxes and seeing whether the results are above, below or the same as chance. He came to the conclusion that known psychics keyed in numbers that were way above chance, and certainly which bore no relation to those keyed in by non-psychics, which obeyed the laws of chance.

Many researchers setting up such experiments have concluded that there is undoubtedly some 'psychic' faculty at work, although they have been at a loss to explain exactly what this might be. My conclusion is that it is no more or less than some kind of unclouded vision which is vouchsafed some people but not others. They can see things that other people can't because they are more simple, because they have less rubbish in their minds, because they are nearer to nature, nearer to their own true selves, because they are less influenced by other people, because they are more self-sufficient.

It seems to me that it is relatively fruitless to speculate on whether this ability resides in brain function or whether it is something wholly non-material in its essence. Obviously, since all we incarnate entities have bodies, all of our skills and talents must be mediated through matter. But that does not necessarily mean that these gifts originate in matter.

It may be possible one day to analyse the brains of clairvoyants and psychics and discover that in some important ways they are wired up differently from those of the rest of us. But that may merely mean that the workings of their minds and emotions causes the brains to be wired up in another manner—in other words, it may not start with the brain. I think it helps if we imagine the brain to be a very complicated computer. It's extremely clever but, like even the most sophisticated computer, it has to be programmed by somebody. The brain, I believe, is powered by whatever is our non-physical essence, the combination of thoughts, emotions and impulses that makes us individual. We want to understand what that non-physical essence is, and whether it has any connection with matter.

At present, the gift of clairvoyance is much like any other creative ability in that as yet, nobody knows exactly where it comes from and why some people should have it and others not. Are clairvoyants tapping into some extra source of information and energy from the universe, or are they accessing their own deepest resources? We don't know and so, up to a point, the clairvoyant ability remains 'unexplained', much as great musical or artistic talent remains unexplained. Nobody has yet offered a convincing explanation as to why some people appear to be born with amazing creative talents, often when there is no background of high achievement in the family. Nobody even knows what can make all the children in one family so different from each other.

In some ways, the clairvoyant ability is much less mysterious than any of these, in that it can be fostered and increased, given an understanding of universal laws, the realization that all actions have consequences and that prices have to be paid for actions which subvert these laws. But as to why some people are more naturally clairvoyant than others—well, perhaps there will never be a satisfactory answer, in that nobody can explain why some people are more beautiful, more gifted, more showered with good fortune than others.

True clairvoyance, though, can be ours, even if we do not ever develop amazing gifts, when we genuinely care about others and when we can see the rest of creation, including animals, as intimately connected to us. Genuine clairvoyants develop their gifts because they are able to love all human beings as though we all belonged to one family.

'Clairvoyance,' wrote the mystic Omraan Mikhael Aivanhov, 'is attained only when the heart begins to love. True clairvoyance resides in the heart.'

MEDIUMSHIP

Here we come to an aspect of the unexplained which is far more mysterious. Very many psychics say they are in direct touch with discarnate entities, disembodied spirits which impart useful information which they can then pass on to their clients. This is known as mediumship.

Very many psychics will say that all their lives they have seen entities that other people don't see, and that these entities are just as real to them as flesh and blood people are to the rest of us. In fact, for many psychics, their world is peopled with hundreds of entities invisible to most people. Because we can't see what these people can, the temptation is to dismiss it all as delusion, hallucinations or actual mental illness. It is well known that schizophrenics hear voices telling them to do things—and also that the 'voices' very often instruct them to highly dangerous or self-destructive activities.

Are there, could there be, such things as disembodied spirits, earthbound spirits, discarnate entities existing on the astral plane—and can some people really get in touch with them and relay information of value to those of us on the earthly plane? To rational people, it all sounds fantastic, beyond belief, and yet to mediums the spirit world is at least as real as any other. Some psychical researchers have drawn an analogy with germs and microbes, reminding us that 100 years ago most doctors and scientists were of the firm opinion that such things did not exist, because they could not be seen with the naked eye. Towards the end of her long life, Florence Nightingale asserted, 'Well, *I* have never seen a germ,' meaning that, in that case, they couldn't exist.

The invention of ever more powerful microscopes has shown us that they do indeed exist, and some psychical researchers believe the day will eventually dawn when spirits, fairies, elemental creatures and ghosts will similarly be able to be shown in pictorial terms. At the moment, the pictorial evidence for elemental beings is slim indeed, although we have to say that all cultures have implicitly believed in them. There are very many fairies, changelings and strange creatures in Shakespeare, and many present-day novelists, from Marquez to Iris Murdoch, deal in magical realism, peopling their contemporary novels with unearthly beings or events. And of course we have to remember that Christians pray to a ghost— the Holy Ghost—and the more fundamental or literal believe in angels, souls and all kinds of discarnate entities. So although we may find it hard to take on board assertions of mediums that they are in touch with 'the spirits', we have to remember that the magical, the strange, is never very far removed from our own experience. Also, what about all the creatures from space which are so popular in comics and films?

Practising mediums use 'spirits' as a means of accessing information that would not be readily obtainable by any other source. At the Spiritual Association of Great Britain, any aspiring medium who wants to work at the society's head-quarters or become a member has to show objective evidence of mediumship, in that they have to relay information they could not have obtained by ordinary sources such as talking to somebody, reading a book or seeing a film. Evidence of communication has to be objectively assessed before any medium is considered to have a genuine gift.

But of course spiritualists are already committed to the notion that there are such things as discarnate entities. It might be argued that they need little persuading of something they believe in already. How is one to convince a sceptic? I don't think there is an easy way—it's something you have to come to gradually, or not at all. There is probably no way whatever of proving to an out and out sceptic that there are such things as spirits or that they can be contacted. Many people no longer believe there is any kind of life or survival beyond physical death. If that is what they firmly believe, then there is little point in setting up complicated experiments to convince them otherwise.

Most practising psychics have told me that it is extremely difficult to persuade 'ordinary' humans that the unseen world is an actual reality. Most people living ordinary humdrum lives regard the idea of another world peopled with vast numbers of invisible beings as too ridiculous a notion to be taken seriously for a minute.

I, too, used to believe that all spirits were so much nonsense and not something that sensible modern people could seriously expect to take on board. I have now changed my views radically, not because I have ever been in contact with a spirit, because I haven't, or because I have had any unusual inform-ation coming from a discarnate source. But I have come to believe that the body is not the only, or perhaps the most important, aspect of human existence, and that physical death is only a transition, not the end. Because I have come to believe in reincarnation—an idea which most modern psychics accept as a fact—it doesn't seem to me all that strange that some people can contact those who have 'passed on' or 'passed over'. You might object, well, it's easy for you to believe there are such things as spirits, which mediums might be able to contact, if you already believe in that kind of thing. But how do you prove it to the rest of us?' The answer is, I can't. I will just let one woman, now a practising psychic, tell her story.

Nora, a teacher who late in life came, somewhat reluctantly, to accept the fact that she must be psychic, said:

Ever since I was a small child, I saw people that nobody else could see. To me, they were as real as anybody else, but once I understood that the grown-ups, and even other children, could not see these people, I started to shut up about it.

But all my life I have heard voices telling me to do things. I came from a very high achieving, rational, scientific kind of family, one which didn't accept this kind of thing at all. When I was at university, I got extremely worried that I heard voices and went to see the university psychologist.

His conclusion was that I was mentally disturbed, probably a schizophrenic. But he couldn't find any other signs of mental disturbance, and so I kept quiet and denied and suppressed it. The thing about these voices was that they were always useful, always inspiring—and they never told me to do anything bad or destructive.

But it was all extremely confusing. I was comforted and nourished by these other entities, whatever they were, and yet they weren't supposed to exist. I then did all the conventional things—qualified as a teacher, got married and had children, and never thought about it for several years until my marriage fell apart, and the voices started playing a part in my life again.

It was at this point that I decided to go to the College of

Psychic Studies in London to try and get to the bottom of it. Now, after many years of attending psychic development courses and practising as a psychic counsellor myself, I have to say I still don't understand the source of these voices.

The reality is that they give me tremendous energy and a host of good feelings. But are they the voices of my higher self, separate discarnate entities or long-dead wise spirits? There is simply no way of proving it at all. But what I can say is that the energy I derive from these spirits, or voices, lasts longer than a cup of tea or a session of psychoanalysis, and that they also help me to help other people.

I feel that without the input of the spirits, I would be no use as a psychic counsellor, or any other type of counsellor. But with them, I find I am given accurate information and guidance. I can't argue with that.

Ivy Northage is a famous British medium who works through her guide Chan. People who have consulted Ivy professionally say that when Chan is guiding her she is quite a different person from when operating 'in her own right'.

Ivy Northage believes that, in order to be psychic, one has to accept the reality of a spiritual world, and to be able to see, hear and feel things which are not readily accessible. The psychic gift, she adds, is a reality to all who possess it, but bridging the gap between the psychic and the non-psychic is extremely difficult. Those who demand a rational, scientific explanation for psychic abilities will probably, says Ivy, not get it, as at the moment such evidence is not available.

All psychics, it seems, have the ability to enter into an altered state of consciousness where they see things that other people don't see. Because of this gift, they are in a special position to help others, because they are seeing themselves as channels for greater wisdom and clarity about situations. They can see patterns that others don't see, give advice that would probably not be forthcoming from an ordinary source.

Another question often asked is: supposing there are such things as spirits, discarnate entities, how come they are so wise and all-knowing, when they may have been wicked, stupid or unenlightened when on earth? How is it that they can suddenly dispense wonderful wisdom the minute they leave the body?

The answer to this is that they can't. Those who believe in the reality of the spirit world, and have investigated it as much as they are able, believe that at least some spirits try to communicate with humans as 'hungry ghosts', that is, disembodied entities who either do not realize they have left the body or who are longing to be attached to a body once again.

There is a popular belief that ghosts are earthbound spirits, people without bodies who are still attached to people or places and cannot leave them. When mediums or psychics try to get in touch with such spirits, they are pulling them back towards the earth and preventing them from reincarnating. The advice from people who have studied such matters is: leave the spirit world severely alone. The 'spirits' who try to contact humans are mischievous, not wise, but wolves in sheep's clothing. The apparent wisdom they dispense is simply an eclectic version of what you can read in any scriptures. There are plenty of perfectly good genuine scriptures and works of philosophy around without having to plough through the reams of virtually unreadable channelled outpourings of obscure American housewives.

The kind of 'spirits' who perpetrate rubbish or nonsense are those who purport to be real people who once lived. Yet, says Joe Fisher, a psychic investigator who made an exhaustive study of this phenomenon in his book *Hungry Ghosts*, information always seems to mysteriously disappear when you try to track these people down. His conclusion is that 'hungry ghosts' do exist, but that they are pretending to be real people for the sake of remaining in contact with the still-living. They choose vulnerable mediums, those who are open to suggestion and who have no great powers of discrimination, to speak through.

Whether this makes any kind of sense, or whether it appears just laughable, will of course depend on your point of view. But since you are actually reading a book about psychic counselling, the presumably you can take these ideas on board, at least in theory. For myself, I'm not sure what I think about 'hungry ghosts'. But it's worth bearing in mind that if you told somebody 100 years ago that you would be able to watch moving pictures of wars in your living-room as they were happening on the other side of the world, they would have looked at you in total astonishment. How could such a thing be possible? And yet, it is.

Presumably, ghosts, whether hungry or not, will not be believed in until they can be represented in no uncertain way, to satisfy the sceptics once and for all. I can now accept that there are unseen forces at work, although whether they are people in disembodied form, or aspects of energy, I can't say. But certainly there is no doubt in my mind that there are in existence sources of energy, healing, light and wisdom that we have hardly begun to tap.

To sum up: the consensus of opinion from all sources I have studied is that intuition, clairvoyance and all the other psychic abilities are part of what is known as the feminine principle, the receptive, passive, non-enquiring principle. It is a mistake to imagine that only women have the 'feminine' principle, and only men possess 'masculine' faculties. The qualities of intuition as well as those of reason, logic and deduction are in all of us and we must make use of them all.

In recent times, the 'feminine' aspect of life has somewhat gone underground, as the masculine principles have come to the fore. Now, it seems, it's time for a reawakening of this other way of looking at things, now that the exclusively masculine view, with its emphasis on control and aggression, is beginning to show us its weak side.

Mediums, or sensitives, are often people who are extremely

vulnerable to impressions, to vibrations coming either from the spirit world (however this may be defined or understood) and they may absorb both the good and the bad. Much of modern science works on the assumption that everything which happens in the universe would happen in the same way if the person conducting the experiment were not there. Everything must be ordered, logical and objective, proceeding as if thoughts, emotions, beliefs and judgements based on partial knowledge did not exist. Leading particle physicists know that this is not true, that all experiments depend, at least in part, on the attitude of the observer, and their beliefs, judgements and emotions can significantly affect the outcome of every experiment. Even to conduct an experiment in the first place depends on having a set of beliefs and no scientist is as detached, critical and objective an observer as they might like to believe. There is, in fact, no such thing as complete objectivity.

Psychic phenomena, as very many researchers know, are often unrepeatable, erratic and unstable. But that does not necessarily mean they do not exist. It does mean, though, that all sorts of fanciful notions can be put forward, as there is nothing objective to measure any statement or assertion against. It must be said, however, that those people who have for themselves had some kind of mystical experience often feel that it is far more real than any other. And any experience which conjures up profound feelings, which changes the way we look at the world, which means we are never the same again, cannot be denied—even if it cannot be repeated.

For many, perhaps most of us, the most dramatic feelings we ever experience are when we are in love. For us, it seems real enough, even if the object of our affections appears perfectly ordinary and unremarkable to other people. For us, they are special—but what laboratory experiment could 'prove' this to us?

The 'unexplainable' will remain unexplainable because the experiences are unique, the phenomena come and go, and there seems no way of pinning them down. The only way to test the reality of the unexplained is to try and experience it for yourself. You may end up believing either that there is nothing in it, or it has nothing to offer you, or you may feel that here is another reality which until now had evaded you.

In the next chapter, we will take a closer look at what psychic counselling is all about and how it may be able to help you.

TWO

WHAT PSYCHIC COUNSELLING IS ALL ABOUT

Psychic counselling is not new. In fact, it is probably the oldest form of counselling and advice there is. Ancient peoples consulted the oracle and the shaman, examined entrails and visited soothsayers and astrologers, often before taking any action whatever.

Seers and prophets were held in high esteem in Biblical times. In the Old Testament, God himself often acted as a direct psychic counsellor, giving advice to the children of Israel on how to conduct their lives, their marriages, their wars and get to the promised land.

In the East, psychic counselling has always flourished and has never lost its importance. Most orthodox Hindus who are contemplating arranged marriages would not dream of doing so without consulting an astrologer to see if the prospective bride and groom are well matched.

In the West, though, psychic counselling more or less faded out with the advent of Christianity, to be replaced by priests and ministers of religion, and later doctors and psychiatrists. In the twentieth century, these people constitute our priestly castes, and are awarded high status by our society, particularly in America, where doctors and therapists are among the highest paid of any profession.

But now that we have become disillusioned with the kind of advice that men of religion can offer, and are fast realizing that medicine and psychiatry also have profound limits, we are rediscovering the oldest form of advice-giving of all—psychic counselling, carried out by those who have become aware of a special gift, rather than having spent years of academic training at a university. In fact, there are no university accredited courses of psychic counselling and none of the 'psychic unfoldment' courses currently on offer have any outside validation from a recognized professional body. That doesn't necessarily mean they are no good. But it does mean that, for the present, psychic counselling remains shrouded in mystery, much as alternative, or complementary, medicine was in the 1960s and 70s, when it was just starting to emerge as a potent force for healing in its own right. After being derided and scorned for years, alternative medicine has now become completely respectable and is even being practised by orthodox doctors. What a change from a few years ago!

Before long, the same should happen to psychic counselling, if we can start to unravel the mystery and suspicion surrounding it, and see it as an effective therapy when properly administered by people who know what they are doing and are fully responsible for the use of their psychic gift.

While it would not be true to say that psychic counselling has yet regained a central place in our lives in the West, it is the case, however, that ever more people are consulting psychics—and not just as a fun or fairground activity, but in all seriousness. So, what can psychics offer that an ordinary counsellor, Citizens' Advice Bureau or doctor can't?

It might be helpful here to say what they *don't* do—at least, the serious ones. They will *not* tell you that you are about to meet a tall dark handsome stranger who will make all your dreams come true or that you will be rich and famous one day. They will not predict that you will win the pools or that all your problems will vanish. Nor will they offer any assurances that your life will be plain sailing and problem-free if you keep consulting them. If, by some chance, you happen to visit a psychic who does tell you such things, beat a hasty retreat, as people who try to tell you that everything in future will be wonderful are not to be trusted.

Similarly, you should not take any notice of those who give you dark warnings of terrible things which are just round the corner. Psychics don't know any more than anybody else what will happen to you. All they can do is to pick up signals, either from the vibrations they receive from you, or from the 'guidance' they receive from whatever source, as to general trends and possibilities in your life.

The main difference between psychic counselling and seeing other kinds of professional is that the advice the psychics give is aimed specifically at you, rather than being generalized advice which might theoretically suit a number of people in your position. A psychic adviser realizes that you are individual, unique, and that what might apply to somebody else may not be suitable for you.

The whole point—or at least the main point—of psychic counselling is that the counsellor will be looking at you, in all your individuality and uniqueness. Also, they will not be looking to benefit from you, as other types of advisor might. For example, if you go to a financial advisor for information on insurance, pension schemes and so on, such a person will try to sell you some kind of scheme which gives him or her a nice commission. The same with lawyers and doctors. Doctors may suggest smears, screens, vaccinations—all because they get more money, or perks from drug companies, for doing so.

Psychic counsellors have to make a living too, of course, but at their best they should be concentrating on how they can help you, rather than how they can help to swell their client list, gain more profits, obtain more commission, achieve more status in the community or enhance their own ego.

Most professionals have large amounts of ego, which is why their advice may be biased or untrustworthy. Genuine psychic counsellors work hard to subdue their own ego and concentrate wholly on their clients. The best ones are able to become 100 per cent receptive to you and themselves may appear to fade away or hardly be there. This attitude—which is not of course present in everybody offering psychic advice—enables them to try and help you sort out what might be best for you, rather than going by the book. Psychic counsellors have no book to go by and no agenda. They are not in the business of telling you what you 'ought' to do, but of helping you to look into your heart and clarify what you really want, what would be the best decision given your particular set of circumstances, character, attitudes and background.

For example, if you are in serious debt and go to see the financial consultant at the Citizens' Advice Bureau, they will look at all your outgoings and income, assess your debts and discuss how you might start reducing the burden. This is sane, sensible advice that the financial expert would give to anybody, whatever their circumstances.

A psychic, by contrast, would probably not ask detailed questions about your financial situation. She knows it is at present your main concern, otherwise you would not be consulting her on this matter. But she would try to find out from you why you have got into such debt, why you felt the need for such self-sabotage and what money means to you— security, a means of exchange, something to be got rid of as quickly as possible or something you have made up your mind not to understand. She might then try to discover what you would like money to do for you and why you feel you haven't got enough or can't seem to earn a decent living. She would try to help you get to the bottom, not just of your present difficulties, but of why you have got yourself into such a situation, and what lessons this particular experience is trying to teach you.

The CAB advisor would probably accept your explanation that you have got into your present state through no fault of your own, that it was hardly down to you that the bank decided to foreclose, that you couldn't sell your house, that your husband or wife decided to leave you or whatever.

A psychic advisor would encourage you to look at the situation quite differently, to start taking responsibility for your financial affairs and to see money as simply a form of exchange, rather than something which is deadly hard to obtain and which keeps slipping away from you. She would probably help you to become 'prosperity conscious' rather than 'poverty conscious' and to inculcate the attitude that if you believe you will always have enough to meet your needs, then this will happen.

I've concentrated on money because this is an area which many people find extremely difficult, possibly more difficult even than relationships. A good piece of advice a psychic counsellor once gave me over money was: whenever considering making a purchase, always ask yourself, would I rather have this than the money? What purpose will this purchase serve and am I prepared to hand over something—a cheque or cash—in exchange for it?

Once you have that attitude, all the guilt and worry you may feel over spending money tends to vanish. Of course, you cannot choose whether or not to pay your bills, but you can always ask yourself whether you would rather have constant hot water and heat and pay a large bill or keep the bill small and be cold. Psychic counsellors, above all, will remind you that you always have a choice over your actions, and even when this doesn't seem apparent, you have a choice over your reactions—you can choose whether to let this particular problem overwhelm you or sort it out to become stronger and more self-reliant in future. When they are doing their proper job, psychic counsellors help you to become stronger in yourself, so that you can begin to take charge of your own life, rather than merely adopting short-term solutions which will bring no long-term gain.

When I go to see my accountant, he advises me on how to maximize my income, how to avoid paying too much tax and how to keep my books in a way that will satisfy the Inland Revenue and Customs and Excise. He cannot—or at least does not—help me to have a better attitude to money so that I stop worrying about it. That's not his job—but it would be the job of a psychic counsellor.

Psychic counselling encourages you as the client to look carefully at yourself, to try and see both destructive and helpful patterns about your life and actions, and put yourself together as a whole, harmonious person. Some psychic counsellors may offer healing, even diagnosing complaints and 'healing your aura' so that your physical health improves, but in fact, all such counselling involves healing in the widest sense of the word, in the sense of helping you to make yourself whole.

Then there is the 'extra ingredient', the factor which makes psychic counselling so exciting and, for some, a little scary at the same time. Your counsellor, unlike the advisor at the Citizens' Advice Bureau, the doctor's or the marriage guidance bureau, may first have to get in touch with a spirit guide or guides and may even go into a trance as well. They may give you information that they have received 'in guidance' and tell you that the words of wisdom they are imparting come not *from* them, but *through* them. In other words, they may claim to be acting as a channel for information from another source, another plane of existence.

All highly peculiar!

Imagine how weird you would feel if when you went to the doctor's surgery, the doctor went into a trance to diagnose your complaint. Perhaps sometimes you think this is exactly what they do—a trance of boredom perhaps or maybe they are daydreaming about going off to golf or deep-sea diving. But not in order to contact unseen entities from 'the other side'.

So on one level, going to see a psychic counsellor is more fun, more exciting, than going to see any other kind of professional advice-giver. You are going to see somebody who professes to have unusual powers, to use spirits or strange powers of divination to help you clarify your life.

Also, a psychic's consulting-room may look very different from that of the average doctor or lawyer. Instead of being filled with NHS posters about vaccinations, stop-smoking clinics and seedy notices about social security benefits, a psychic's consulting-room is likely to be filled with crystals, incense sticks, New Age music and pleasing astrological and symbolic pictures. The ambience is different, and instantly it makes you feel special, rather than just number 13 on the waiting list that day.

But if going to see a psychic is more fun, it can also be far more nerve-racking than consulting an ordinary professional.

This is because most of us are far removed from any spiritual dimension in our lives these days. Going to church on Sundays, for the few who still do, is hardly an exotic experience. But going to a psychic, at least for the first time, is to take a step into an unknown world. You do not know what will happen, or, as important, how you might react to the sheer strangeness of it all.

On my first visit to a psychic counsellor, a middle-aged woman who used crystals, I was very nervous indeed. I had no idea what might happen, what she might do or how I might react. I arrived at the psychic's house at about eight in the morning and left after midday. During all those hours, I had no sensation of time passing and I was in what felt like suspended animation, not exactly hypnotized, but certainly in a state of altered consciousness.

As the crystals were passed about a foot over my body as I lay on a soft sofa, a cold shudder ran through me. Even though at the time I was extremely sceptical about crystals and crystal healing, I could not deny the reality of that shiver. For most of the time during the session, I had no idea what I might be going to say next and I was surprised to discover that very strong and disturbing feelings came to the surface. I began to learn that there were intensely painful aspects of my life which I had not wanted to address and that, far from being the serene, peaceful and controlled person I had imagined, I was actually a mass of unresolved tensions, fears and problems.

The psychic counsellor did not tell me this, but I began to realize it for myself, and understand that this venture was an important step on a journey to self-discovery, a journey which eventually helped me to become stronger and more self-reliant, and also started to open my eyes to a wider perspective, a new way of looking at things.

I emerged from the session into blinding midday light, and sat in a cafe feeling stunned and dazed. I had only gone to see this counsellor in a spirit of investigation, not really to find out more about myself, and I discovered that the consultation had brought to the surface a mass of strong and uncomfortable feelings which I had tried to bury over the years. It also left me with the realization that in some ways I had been very closed-minded and had dismissed the psychic world as being so much nonsense and chicanery without having any real idea of what it was about.

My first session had left me with such very strong feelings and emotions—not *all* painful I must admit—that I felt I wanted to get to the bottom of it all. Since then, I have visited a number of psychic consultants, both for my own therapy and for the purposes of research. I have discovered that they vary enormously and use a wide spectrum of approaches. With some, you will sit opposite them in a chair. Others might prefer you to lie down on a couch or bed. Some talk, while you listen. Others draw you out and expect you to do most of the talking. There are no hard and fast rules, and most psychics develop over the years the approach which seems to suit them best.

In Chapter 5, we will try to establish some ground-rules for visiting psychic counsellors and talk about what happens from the clients' point of view. For the rest of this chapter, professional psychic counsellors tell how they operate—and how they use their psychic faculties to help their clients.

Brenda Marshall has for very many years been associated with the College of Psychic Studies, established in 1881 and situated in South Kensington, London. A past president of the society, she now spends most of her time counselling individuals.

She said:

The whole point of psychic counselling, when it works well, is that it gets to the root of the problem quicker than might be possible by other means. Because genuine psychics are in communication with other levels of consciousness, they can use their intuition and telepathy to help people, rather than having to ask laborious questions.

At its heart, psychic counselling can only be used to

help a person's spiritual, rather than material, welfare.
I feel that such counselling is only really appropriate if
somebody feels they have come to a crossroads and need
guidance on their own spiritual health. In order to gain
from psychic counselling, people have to have become
aware of the spiritual dimension.

This does not, Brenda emphasized, mean that they have to
believe in ghosts, spirits or other discarnate entities, but to
realize that there may be important aspects of life which do not
involve the material dimension. Therefore, questions such as
'Will I be rich?' 'Will I meet the man of my dreams?' 'Will I win
the pools?' are inappropriate reasons for wanting guidance
from a psychic.

Brenda continued:

Obviously we are living in the material world and
material welfare cannot be ignored. But we who use the
psychic approach are more concerned with non-material
values. Basically, the message comes down to something
as simple as 'Love thy neighbour as thyself'.

People have to be prepared not to hurt others, and
although psychic gifts can be used to send curses to other
people and do them down, this is not the kind of
approach that any psychic offering genuine help would
take.

At the College, we always respect the free will of
individuals, and never try to persuade them to any
particular course of action. One important way of helping
people with a particular problem is that we try to
encourage them to see it as a lesson which their higher
self is trying to teach them. As psychics, we try to use our
own higher selves to guide clients and we speak to their
own highest selves. In true psychic guidance, the higher
self of both the psychic and the client should be in
communication.

Any psychically gifted person who continually bears this in mind cannot do much harm, Brenda says. Probably the majority of people visit a psychic counsellor not out of idle curiosity but because they have recently suffered a bereavement and want some kind of evidence of survival, some kind of reassurance that, in spite of their previous convictions, physical death cannot be all. They want reassurance that their beloved person has not been snatched away from them in vain.

In this case, some mediums may try to give such evidence by contacting the recently departed person, while others may offer spiritual counselling and guidance.

Brenda said:

For many people, going to see a medium provides a starting-point for a spiritual journey, doing their own reading and research and looking at the body of evidence for spiritual reality. Although there is a lot of scepticism, and people *should* be sceptical when enquiring into psychic matters, the fact is that there have been 110 years of serious research into the subject now, and it cannot all be easily dismissed.

Our approach is not to do or say anything which would lose the respect of a fair-minded sceptic. We are not saying we have all the answers, but even the most hardened materialist has to see now that the world is on a crash course to disaster unless we are very careful. Anybody who has enough sensitivity to be awakened these days is awakened. When we are in extremely comfortable circumstances we may sail on blithely. It is usually only when people are at some kind of crossroads or feel there is a serious gap in their lives that they may consult a psychic.

People will often go to see a psychic when they are truly desperate, and most psychic counsellors will see a large number of clients who are in the depths of depression, unhappiness or misery, who feel that life has no longer any purpose or meaning. It is, very often, some truly hideous misfortune which brings people to a psychic counsellor. In their normal, ordinary lives, such a step would probably never even be considered.

But of course, you do not have to have a serious problem, or even a problem at all, to visit a psychic. You can simply be looking for a new angle, a new approach to your life.

Philippe Raynaud is a Frenchman who trained as a lawyer and accountant before becoming a psychic counsellor 10 years ago. He describes his approach:

I sit down and use crystals to focus attention. Then I close my eyes and connect to somebody's energy. Before long, things start to come to me and suddenly I seem to remember all sorts of things about them. It's as if I already know about them, at some level, and it just has to come up to the surface.

I am not in contact with any spirit guides as far as I know, but I tune into my own intuition. I find that the more I tune into it, the more I'm right in predicting or helping people get to the heart of what is troubling them. But sometimes, I must say, I wonder whether I *am* tuning into spirits of some kind. I certainly sometimes see people standing behind my clients, when I know there's nobody actually there. When talking with a client, I say what comes into my head, but sometimes I wonder why it does come in. Often, I haven't got a clue beforehand. It often seems a bit like reciting a poem which I have never consciously learned, but which comes to me as I carry on.

I think that many people get to a certain stage in life where they are muddled up and don't see any way out of their situation. I tell people why they are in their particular difficulties and offer guidance as to how they might be able to get out of it. I am not a fortune-teller by any means and I insist on helping people make their own decisions in life. It seems to me that the more I trust, the more comes up and the more accurate I become.

It is, as I see it, a big responsibility to be a psychic. People think you are very different from them, but you're not. All that happens is that you are seeing things at a different level, a level where everything connects up and forms patterns.

Philippe believes that psychic counselling works best when ordinarily healthy people have a particular problem or are just seeking some guidance and reassurance in their lives, rather than for those who may be mentally ill or have a diagnosable psychiatric disorder.

He says:

Psychoanalysis, as I see it, is for those with serious lifelong problems. Many people come to me simply because they are curious and want to know why their life has taken a particular turn or why things don't seem to be going right. My own belief about the future, free will and so on is that our destiny is mapped out, but that we can change the disc. For instance, you may be on a train going to Bristol, and you can't avoid that, but you can get out at any station along the way. You don't have to go to Bristol simply because you are on that train. But as long as you stay on that same journey, you have to go to the end.

I believe my main function as a psychic counsellor is to help people see more clearly what they ought to do. Some people imagine that as I used to be an accountant, I will give financial advice from a psychic point of view. But for me, as for most psychics, our consciousness is not in money and that's why we are not rich. You won't find many practising psychics who are actually poor. Most of us have a comfortable lifestyle but we are not wealthy because our minds are not primarily focused on making money. It's simply not where we put our energy.

As psychic counselling works so much more quickly than standard counselling, many people find that one session is enough. In any case, the first session will be the major one, establishing what the problem is.

People have to feel ready to come to a psychic counsellor and most of the input has to come from them. I feel very strongly about what I do and take it extremely seriously.

Philippe Raynaud believes that the openness or otherwise of the client makes a good deal of difference to the outcome of the sitting.

If people disbelieve it makes connecting extremely difficult. I feel that my psychic gift has enabled me to see why people are the way they are and also to remind them that things which look terrible when they happen may actually be the best thing. Taking the long view is important and one of my jobs is to help people look at their situations from a wider perspective.

In particular, Philippe Raynaud reckons he can help people to sort out patterns in their lives and enable them to see why they often repeat actions which are not perhaps serving their best interests.

People often don't realize they are enacting patterns or that when they are dissatisfied with their partners— dissatisfaction with relationships is one major reason for seeing a psychic counsellor—they are actually dovetailing patterns. Mostly, we hate in other people what we hate in ourselves, which is why we recognize and respond to it. There is almost always a lot to unravel in unhappy relationships, but until people can see for themselves how they may have contributed to the destructive patterns, they will just go on repeating them with new partners.

I feel that my main job is to help people open their eyes to what is really going on in their lives and to take responsibility for what is happening. When people can see the

patterns they have been creating, they can often then
start to break them and embark on healthier relationships.

Dr Lisa Sand is an unusual psychic counsellor in that she is a
qualified psychiatrist. Ever since the late 1970s, she has been
working closely with a medium, Inga Hooper, to help people in
a way she feels standard psychiatry cannot touch.

> Over the years I worked in conventional psychiatry, I
> came to realize that most people worked by the book
> rather than offering any real insights. I gradually became
> aware of other dimensions and had a number of psychic
> experiences myself. Then I met up with Inga and together
> we can work to help people in a way that would be
> impossible by ourselves.
>
> I would say that through mediumistic counselling we
> can accomplish more in three hours than traditional
> psychiatry can achieve in six years. We don't take on just
> anybody but reserve our time for those people who have
> a genuine sense of purpose. We feel we are working
> closely with Jung in the spirit world and we believe firmly
> in reincarnation.
>
> Some people come to us out of curiosity, but most want
> to gain some clarity and purpose to their lives. They have
> to feel ready to come and so would not be 'referred' in the
> way that a doctor might refer a patient to a psychiatrist,
> for example. Unless people feel themselves ready for
> psychic guidance, there is nothing that we can offer them
> and we are all just wasting our time.

Veronica Stephenson, who sees clients at a residential centre in
northern Scotland, feels she combines psychotherapy with a
psychic approach:

> I would describe the kind of counselling I do as intuitive.
> The psychic gift comes not so much in my case from
> tuning into spirit guides as being able to get on to my

clients' wavelength and see things from their point of view. Sometimes I am also able to see, or visualize, their past lives while we are working on their present problems. I try to establish a psychic link with my patients and rely on my intuition to ask the right questions. I think the secret of helping people face themselves and sort out their lives is to know when to probe and when not to probe. You have to have patience, and you certainly get better with practice.

Like all gifts, psychic abilities improve the more you use them. There is certainly a place for conventional psychotherapy and psychoanalysis in taking things apart, but you have to be careful to build them up as well, and this is where psychic abilities help. The ability to relate to people's pains and strengths draws something special out of the session and provides a kind of spiritual alchemy.

I think the answer to 'Am I psychic?' is 'How much do I care about people? Am I able to put myself in the other person's shoes and imagine what their situation must be like?' Obviously I as a therapist can't have gone through every single experience my patients bring to me but I can understand what it is like to be afraid, to be on the receiving end of violence and lose control. There's always some way I can relate, and I need to be able to empathize and have imagination.

Veronica feels that anybody who is interested in undertaking this kind of work has to have the stamina and strength to be able to deal with other people's problems without absorbing them and so risking suffering from burn-out.

If you absorb the problems into yourself, you can't keep yourself strong. I feel for my clients but I have to remain detached. I do sometimes weep with them, but I don't wallow in their problems, as this doesn't help anybody at all. It is also essential to be able to shut down and recharge the batteries. Basically, I feel it's all to do with love—loving oneself, loving others and feeling connected to every human being. I don't think any effective psychic counselling can be accomplished without love.

This is just a small selection of the ways in which psychic counsellors work. In this chapter, I have concentrated on some of the more familiar, counselling aspects of it, and explaining how they may differ from conventional therapy and advice. But as we all know, the world of psychic matters uses many arcane and unusual terms which may convey little or no meaning to somebody new to this way of working. What, for instance are auras? What part do the mysterious tarot cards play? What are chakras? What does it mean to 'close down' and 'open up'? Are these terms so much meaningless mumbo-jumbo, used to make psychic counselling appear more mysterious and esoteric than, really, it need be?

In the next chapter we will explore all these areas and discuss how they may help, or hinder, you, when seeking advice from a psychic.

THREE

THE VAST FIELD OF
PSYCHIC COUNSELLING

As we have seen in the previous chapter, people who have identified psychic gifts in themselves have very varied ways of working. To the beginner putting a cautious toe into the field, it may all sound extremely mysterious.

But there is more mystery to come. Going to see a psychic counsellor will open up a whole new world for you and ask you to take on board things which cannot be seen or easily evaluated. You will come into contact with such phenomena as auras, chakras, pendulums, dowsing, psychometry, past-life therapy...

What does it all mean—if anything? Can you, as a sane, sensible, rational individual, take any of it seriously? My answer is yes, but it is only when armed with knowledge and information that you can evaluate it all. You may find that aura and chakra readings are not for you—but until you understand what they are all about, you have no way of knowing.

This chapter will give an alphabetical run-down of the aids and terms used in psychic counselling, with the aim of demystifying it and so enabling you to make some kind of sense of it all and work out what might appeal to you. Some people like a very plain, no-nonsense approach, where the counsellor dresses in ordinary clothes, sits in an ordinary chair in an ordinary room and talks to you without going into a trance, seeing spirits behind you or contacting the dead. Other people may prefer to see a counsellor who offers them an exotic experience at the same time as the advice. In this way, psychic counselling is a bit like the great variety of approaches within the Christian church: you can go to a highly ornate Greek Orthodox or Catholic church and wallow in a sensuous experience at the same time as getting nearer to God. Or you can go to the other extreme and attend a Quaker meeting-house which is perfectly plain and simple, and everybody has an equal chance to speak and be heard.

The approach which suits you will be partly a matter of your own personality and partly a matter of why you are interested in seeing a psychic counsellor in the first place: do you simply want information or are you interested in having a heady experience at the same time?

Only you can decide. In the meantime, here is a handy guide to the enormous and ever-expanding range of psychic counselling.

AKASHIC RECORDS

The Akashic Record is supposed to be the psychic record or book of every event which has ever happened in the history of the world. 'Akashic' is a Sanskrit word which means 'etheric substance'.

Some psychics help their clients by tuning into the Akashic Records, and 'reading your book'. This gives them information on your past lives and how they have a bearing on your present.

The thing is, do such people really tap into ancient records existing in the non-material sense on the ethereal plane, or are they just having you on? Unfortunately, there is no real way of knowing. All you can do is to see whether what they say makes any sense to you or sheds any light on your present circumstances.

There is no doubt that an Akashic Record reading is a highly exotic experience. It may be, though, that the psychic is simply picking up what sort of person you are and is describing past lives which seem to match up in some way to your present incarnation. It goes perhaps without saying that all psychics who use the Akashic Record approach believe firmly in reincarnation and maintain that all humans have souls which lead them into one incarnation after another for the purpose of learning important lessons. It is rather similar to Jung's idea of the universal unconscious, although a psychic using this method will apply it directly to you.

I would say, from personal experience of having an Akashic Record reading, that people who use this approach are completely sincere in what they are doing. They firmly believe they are tapping into this universal memory and that they have, for some reason, been given special dispensation to read the Akashic book. The only way of evaluating it is to ask whether it yields valuable information which would have been hard to come by in any other way.

My own Akashic Record consultation brought home to me that, throughout the ages, I had always been strong, independent and non family-minded. The psychic, Lee Ward, may have picked all this up just from looking at me, but somehow, the information that I had always been like this, through several incarnations of varying discomfort and difficulty, strengthened my resolve to try and remain my own person, and not be too influenced by society's prevailing norms and beliefs.

Usually, psychics who give Akashic Record readings will not ask you too many questions about yourself, but will look straight into your eyes and then start reeling off information. There is no guarantee that the reading will illuminate everything, or even anything, but it is unlikely to do any harm.

This form of psychic counselling is becoming ever more popular as more people in the West take on board the idea that we probably have more than one physical incarnation.

ASTRAL BODY

I think it is safe to say that all practising psychics believe that there is more to us than just the physical body. We all possess, they say, a number of subtle bodies—the astral, etheric and spiritual bodies. Most offer no evidence for this belief, except that they can 'see' them, whereas a doctor, or psychiatrist, or even your dearest lover or partner can't. During a counselling session, a psychic or medium will be able to see your astral body and tap into it to gain extra sources of information.

At night, say psychics, we leave our physical bodies while our astral bodies take over and separate themselves from the physical body. They can, though, go back into the physical at any time—such as when we wake up, or are rudely awakened by an alarm clock or somebody snoring. When we die, we become only astral, or etheric, as the physical body dies and decomposes or is burnt.

As an understanding of the various subtle bodies is so much an integral part of psychic counselling, it is pointless to ask whether it makes any sense. If you're a psychic, you see these bodies, if you're not, you don't—and that's all there is to say. To psychics, they are as real as the flesh-and-blood body in front of them—in some cases, *more* real.

What is the objective evidence for their existence? I turned to my old friend electrical engineer Professor Arthur Ellison for some enlightenment. His view is that mediums are among the most honest and genuine people he has ever met, and that if they say astral bodies exist, then they are perfectly sincere. However, he adds that as they are not scientists, and are frequently not educated people in the accepted sense, the claims they make for subtle bodies may be too literal to be accepted readily by the rest of us.

He feels that psychics tend to 'dramatize' what they see and have a greater ability than most of us to conjure up an actual presence for what for others may simply be an impression—for example, what we call a foreboding 'atmosphere' may be for a psychic an actual ghost. They put thoughts into a kind of physical form and seeing the astral body may be just such a literalization of a thought or impression.

So when psychics 'see' our astral bodies, they are picking up some 'essence' about us which is not visible to ordinary eyes. Whereas you or I may get a strong feeling about somebody, a psychic may see two or three actual bodies, each representing a different aspect of the same person. For a psychic, a client's spiritual outlook may be represented by an actual being of light, their emotions by a denser being and so on.

This form of representation is not unique to psychics. Many poets, writers and painters have represented states of mind as actual people or monsters. One only has to think of John Bunyan's *Pilgrim's Progress*, where we meet Mr Worldly-Wiseman, Apollyon, Good Will, Hope and Faithful. Personifications of emotions, attitudes and beliefs are familiar as literary devices, and it may be that psychics are using a similar creative ability.

Certainly, no scientist has ever been able to devise an experiment which 'proves' there are such things as astral bodies. But as ever more people seem to have out-of-the-body experiences, we cannot entirely dismiss the idea of another type of body. But considerations as to whether it has any kind of physical form or can actually be seen with the physical eye remain open to question.

But really, does it matter? If scientific investigations one day prove, or disprove, the reality of an astral body, will it make any difference? As psychic counselling proceeds on the assumption that we do have these subtle bodies, whether visible or not, unless you feel comfortable with taking the concept on board, you will probably not like the idea of this form of counselling anyway.

ASTROLOGY

Astrology is probably the best known of all psychic arts. Most, if not all, people nowadays know their star sign and have some idea what sort of character it indicates. Sometimes this seems to be completely accurate and in other cases it appears to bear no relation whatever to the person. For instance, my former husband, two sons and myself once watched an astrology video 'for intelligent people' made by the well-known psychologist and astrologer Liz Greene. We found that my husband's and two sons' character readings were astonishingly accurate, but mine was not me at all.

Because no astrological reading I have ever had has been at all accurate, I have misgivings about it, although I know that very many people have benefited. Again, so long as the psychic has your best interests at heart, there is probably no actual harm in it, although be careful of going by a too literal interpretation.

There is, of course, a vast difference between the generalized advice given in newspaper and magazine 'stars', and an individual reading given by a professional astrologer. In order to give an accurate reading, the astrologer needs to know your exact time and place of birth so that a birth chart can be drawn up.

Your birth chart is a map of the position of the planets as seen at the exact time of your birth and, according to astrologers, is a profound source of insight into your character, inclinations, potential and likelihood of compatibility with other people. Everybody's birth chart is individual, and an astrological reading should relate to you and nobody else. Astrology is basically a system of interpreting the movements of the planets, which are thought to be correlated to human thoughts, character and behaviour.

These days, an increasing number of astrologers work by computer, which saves the effort of painstakingly drawing up birth charts, and which makes the whole procedure much quicker.

Psychologist Mary Russell uses astrological charts of clients to help her gain a wider perspective on what is going on in their lives, and give her insights into their character, emotions, mental and physical health. She says:

> I find astrology a wonderful tool. As I'm drawing up the chart I get ideas about problems and resolutions, and a strong feeling from other levels of reality about what a particular client might need.
>
> I don't go into a state of altered consciousness when I see clients, and I don't use crystals, but I find that horoscopes can be a very accurate guide.

The point about astrology is not that 'the stars' exactly influence your life, but that there is a strong correlation between celestial and terrestrial events. It is the astrologer's job to be able to interpret these accurately and come up with information which will be of use to you. The rationale behind astrology is that the universe is seen as an indivisible whole whereby everything is interconnected and nothing is left to chance.

So the position of the planets at the moment of your birth—considered to be when the umbilical cord is cut—do not cause the patterns of your life, but merely correspond. You have choice of actions and you retain free will. Your birth chart indicates strengths and weaknesses of character, but what you do with the qualities bestowed on you is your choice. The birth chart describes your potential, but does not say how you will use that potential.

Astrology works on the principle of the 'great chain of being', which means that nothing is separate and that everything which happens is a link between heaven and earth. Many of the best astrologers are now also trained in Jungian psychology, which is based on the idea of the universal unconscious, and they are able to bring the two disciplines together, so that the ancient art of divination and prediction ties up with the modern practice of psychology.

This is a relatively new development. Until the 1970s, most psychologists dismissed astrology as so much quackery and fakery. They argued that astronomical knowledge had made nonsense of ancient astrological charts, which assumed the sun went around the earth. But then the work of Michel Gauquelin, a French psychologist and statistician, threw them into confusion.

Dr Gauquelin undertook painstaking research to see whether there was any correlation between the birth charts of certain famous people and their occupations. At the time of instigating the research, he was convinced that astrology was so much nonsense, but to his surprise, he discovered that sports champions were born when Mars was in a particular position, that famous actors had Jupiter in the ascendant, and that Saturn was auspicious for eminent doctors and scientists. Dr Gauquelin's research appeared to confirm what the ancients had been saying and encouraged other psychologists to instigate their own research projects.

The astrologer Jeff Mayo participated with Professor Hans Eysenck, of the Institute of Psychiatry in London, in an experiment designed to show whether extroverts and introverts were born in particular signs of the zodiac. They compiled a highly complicated introversion–extroversion questionnaire and sent it to 2,324 participants in 1975. The results of this exhaustive study showed that those born with water signs (Cancer, Scorpio and Pisces) prominent in their birth chart tended more to emotionalism and neuroticism than people born under any of the other signs, thus appearing to validate an ancient astrological theory. People born under Aries, Gemini, Leo, Libra, Sagittarius and Aquarius tended towards extroversion, whereas those born under Taurus, Cancer, Virgo, Scorpio, Capricorn and Pisces were more likely to be introverts.

Commenting on the results of this study, Professor Eysenck said:

I must admit that this was a great surprise to me...my instinctive scepticism and dislike of anything mystical had led me to expect unrelieved failure from any investigations of astrological predictions. To find some solid fact in the astrological field was surprising and not entirely welcome...

Perhaps our arrogance has been misplaced: there may indeed be more things in heaven and earth than we have dreamed of.

Even though scientific experiments are increasingly validating the worth of astrology, it is worth pointing out that drawing up birth charts, and having a detailed knowledge of the position of the planets and the solar system, are only *tools*. Like any other means of amplification, astrological information has to be interpreted in an intuitive way. Also, like other psychic aids, it is not infallible, and mistakes can be made.

It is best to use astrology as a guide to your character and potential, rather than the last word.

AURAS

Most, if not all, psychics see 'auras' around people, a host of coloured lights rather like a halo surrounding the entire body. Some psychics make a speciality of aura cleansing and healing. When people are in good health physically and mentally, they say, the aura around them is clear, healthy and bright. But when they are ill or troubled, it becomes grey, cloudy and muddy-looking. Again, no photography or other pictorial representation has convincingly shown the sceptic that there is such a thing as the aura, or that it has any kind of physical form or colouring.

From ancient times, though, people have been represented with auras around them. Haloes in Christian art are representations of auras, even though they are usually drawn only around the head. Some pictures of Christ, however, show him with a band of light around his whole body and angels are often represented as being surrounded by light.

In sacred art, those with haloes or auras are seen as being especially holy people, and I have known scientists and biologists who to this day see auras around genuinely spiritual people. But psychics see auras around everybody.

Part of the training of mediums, in psychic unfoldment classes, is to enable them to see these auras and to interpret them. Spiritual healers will see a shadow on the aura in the place where the illness or disease has manifested itself, and will heal by visualizing it to go away and become clear.

In his book *Understanding Auras*, Joseph Ostrom explains the phenomenon as a collection of electro-magnetic energies of varying densities which are coming from the various bodies— physical, mental, astral and etheric. These particles of energy are suspended around the body in an oval-shaped field.

For somebody who has never seen an aura, this perhaps has to be taken on trust, but there is no doubt that most psychics and mediums do see auras as clearly as they perceive eyes, ears, faces and physical bodies.

It may be, says Arthur Ellison, that psychics' brains are wired up in ways that are somehow different from the rest of us, and it is this unusual wiring which enables them to see things that other people can't. It is the case, though, that many 'ordinary' people can see things which aren't visible to others when they go into altered states of consciousness by using drugs, hypnosis or prolonged meditation or fasting. People at the peak of a meditative experience often see bright blue lights when no such lights exist or are conscious of millions of lights all around them when the day is dark and cloudy. The difference between these experiences, which tend to occur only occasionally, and those of psychics, is that psychics see them all the time.

There is certainly nothing to be afraid of in visiting a psychic who talks about your aura, and tells you, or draws for you, what they see. To a psychic, an aura conveys an emotional state as accurately as the most complicated questionnaire, and can diagnose disease far more sensitively than any tool an ordinary doctor might have. Indeed, there are many cases on record of where a psychic has 'seen' a disease by reading the aura, and startled doctors.

The accuracy with which a psychic sees and interprets your aura may vary considerably but the certainty is that they will always see you surrounded by light and shade.

All of us have various energies emanating from us, and it is not difficult for anybody to understand that some people give off favourable vibes, while others make you feel uncomfortable and ill at ease. As we have seen, to a psychic, these energies appear in an almost physical form. Those who make you feel uneasy may be liars, cheats, destructive or negative people, and this will show up in their aura as dark, cloudy emanations. By contrast, light, happy, positive people will have bright and colourful auras. Aura counselling, or healing, will help you to remove the dark patches and shine up your aura. Or at least, that is the promise.

If you proceed with psychic counselling you too may be able to see auras around people, and this will help you to know which should be avoided and which will have a positive influence for you. It all comes down eventually to intuition— auras may be no more or less than the ability to enable the intangible to become tangible, in some way. They may be a convenient way of describing the increased perception which comes with psychic awareness.

AUTOMATIC WRITING

Many books on psychical research will have pictures of wavy, almost illiterate-looking writing which purports to be 'automatic' and come from some kind of spirit guide.

Automatic writing does not seem to be as popular as it was, although some mediums and psychics still use it. Most professional writers have actually experienced a kind of automatic writing or, these days perhaps, automatic word-processing, when their hand seems guided by something unseen and beyond them. The highly prolific children's writer Enid Blyton used sometimes to look at what she had just written and say, 'Whatever's that? I'd never have thought of it.' Professional writers often feel that what they are writing is being dictated to them and all they have to do is get it down. It's as if something takes over, something of which they are not entirely conscious. But such 'inspiration' is no indicator of literary worth. Critics of Enid Blyton's work have dismissed even her most inspired stories as crude, racist and sexist.

Is there a difference between what some professional writers experience as 'inspiration', where they are guided by an unseen hand, and the kind of automatic writing practised by some psychics?

Automatic writing can be regarded as a way of transferring information from the unconscious to the conscious, without the conscious mind being involved in the process. The unconscious mind controls the hand which is producing the writing, or maybe the drawing.

The healer Matthew Manning produced many examples of automatic writing and painting when a schoolboy, always in the style of somebody who had 'passed over'. He could reproduce Aubrey Beardsley and Picasso through the unconscious, although he himself had very little drawing ability at all.

Many mediums believe that when they are producing automatic writing or drawing, the hand of an unseen spirit guide is actually at work and they are simply being used as a physical channel, as the entity of course has no body and cannot communicate directly with clients.

The only way to regard automatic writing and drawing is to assess its quality. With most automatic writing, the words flow into one another and have a slightly dreamy, faraway look. One famous example of automatic writing is where the medium Geraldine Cummins wrote the plot of a W. B. Yeats book through automatic writing when in his presence. Most of the stuff that 'comes through', however, is of low quality and most psychic drawings I have seen have no great artistic merit. Figures usually look more like 'Wanted' posters, stiff and lifeless, than animated human beings. I have never yet seen any examples of automatic writing which are calligraphically attractive. Nor have I read any which make much sense, are of a high order of literary merit, or which dispense any unusual wisdom or insight.

The phenomenon of automatic writing and drawing indicates an aspect of psychics and mediums that is not always appreciated: even if material is channelled through the medium by some discarnate entity, it has to be passed through the brain cells and intelligence of the channel. Therefore, you are likely only to get communications which are on the same intellectual level as the psychic. If the psychic is highly intelligent and sensitive, you are likely to get useful stuff, otherwise, it is probably banal and second-rate.

The mystical genius William Blake firmly believed his work was guided by an unseen hand, but then Barbara Cartland believes God gives her plots and helps her write her hundreds of romantic novels, which not even Dame Barbara's most fervent admirers could call classic literature.

CARTOMANCY

This is the use of cards for divination or character reading. Many psychics still use cards, either ordinary playing cards or the more mysterious tarot deck. Although the tarot seems esoteric and perhaps slightly scary, there is a close similarity between the two sets of cards. With the tarot, the swords are clubs, the cups are hearts, the pentacles are diamonds and the wands are spades.

If you go to see a psychic who uses cards, you will usually be asked to shuffle the pack and then ask questions as the psychic deals out the cards. Good cartomancers then use their powers of intuition or ESP to give you the answers. Both ordinary playing cards and the tarot have built up layers and layers of meaning over the centuries, and somebody using cards will be able to interpret things individually for you while bearing in mind the traditional meanings of the cards in the pack.

Psychic Murry Hope, who uses cards with her clients, said:

Reading cards is quite a complicated business and takes a long time to learn. My feeling is that cards should be used only for serious purposes and never for fun, or for scaring people.

A card reading, like any other psychic aid, depends very much on the skill of the individual reader. It doesn't work like an exact science and an accurate reading includes being able to sum up the character of the person in front of you.

She believes that although card reading can be learned, it is mostly a gift.

'Through the pack,' she said, 'you can tell fortunes, meditate, and help people with their mental and physical health. Your job as the psychic is to interpret the symbols and divine what is going on in the client's subconscious mind.'

The client has to hold the pack to let their vibrations pass into the cards, and the psychic then takes them back to deal them into, usually, a circle.

'Although the cards have definite symbols, it is up to me to see how these might apply to the individual in front of me, as all are capable of a variety of interpretations.'

For instance, in the tarot pack, turning up a sword may mean cutting off from the past, the loss of a friend or relative, or a new and exciting departure. 'We know it means some sort of cutting off,' Murry said, 'but the interpretation has to be relevant to the person in front of you.'

No card reading can be guaranteed to be 100 per cent accurate. I have been for card readings which have been so completely inaccurate they bore no relation to me or my circumstances at all, and others which seemed uncannily prescient. It probably all comes down in the end to the gift of the psychic. As with other psychic aids, there is no inherent magic in cards, but they can help to focus and amplify intuitive abilities for some people.

CHAKRAS

These are the ancient 'energy centres' supposed to be in every human, although no instrument has so far been able to show them. There are seven main chakras altogether: the root chakra (situated in the genitals), the sacral chakra (in the abdomen), the solar plexus, the heart, the throat, the 'third eye' and the crown (at the top of the head).

In yoga practice, the idea is to bring energy, known as kundalini, from the root to the crown.

Some psychics practise chakra healing, concentrating on unblocking these energy sources on the assumption that much illness and emotional disturbance is caused by energy blockage in these areas. If you go to a psychic, it is quite likely that he or she will talk about 'unblocking the chakras' as part of the healing process. This is achieved by visualizing energy flowing freely through the body.

CHANNELLING

Channelling is the American term for mediumship, and there is now a vast amount of 'channelled' literature purporting to come straight from long-dead entities on other planes. Many psychics believe that they act as mediums, or channels, for other levels of reality, or so that spirits and discarnate entities can speak through them.

There seems little doubt that some people are extremely 'open' to this kind of communication, although whether it comes from their own unconscious mind, whether they are tapping into the unconscious mind of their clients, whether spirits really do speak through them or what, has never been conclusively established. All we can be sure about, from the body of evidence collected on the subject so far, is that psychics definitely do gain extra energy and insights when their spirit guides—or whatever—are in operation. They do hear voices and sometimes see people.

Whether or not these voices or people really exist in a sense doesn't matter, because what is important is whether the psychic is shedding light on some perverse or difficult problem. If the 'spirits' help in this work, then who's to say they don't exist? Very many people say, even nowadays, that they hear God speaking directly to them, or that they get a 'call' from Jesus. And certainly not all of these people can be called mentally ill.

Most practising psychics are eminently sensible and sane people—one only has to pay a visit to the British College of Psychic Studies to discover how normal they are—but they are somehow in touch with another dimension. Perhaps they give it a name and form that the rest of us can't see—but that may be our blindness, rather than their delusion.

This century has seen a vast amount of 'channelled' literature—words of wisdom and advice purporting to come from wise entities on the astral plane. For some reason, channelling large amounts of written material seems to be mainly an American phenomenon, with names like Jane Roberts and her 'Seth' books, and A Course in Miracles, the best-selling book published in 1975 and containing material channelled by Helen Cohn Schucman, a psychologist employed at the Psychiatry Department of Columbia University in New York.

Other modern channels have been Eileen Caddy, Dorothy MacLean and David Spangler from Findhorn in Scotland, J. Z. Knight and her 'Ramtha' channellings, and Jach Pursel and 'Lazaris'. Most of the entities contacted by American channels are people who were never famous in their physical incarnations, but who appear to be able to dispense an inexhaustible supply of wisdom now they are disembodied.

We do not know whether such material 'really' comes from an outside channelled source or whether it is some externalization of an aspect of the person doing the channelling. We can only ask: does the channel speak wisdom or nonsense and is this kind of information available from more normal sources?

CLAIRAUDIENCE

This is the term given to the facility of being able to hear what is being said by somebody who no longer has a body. How it is literally possible to hear something said by a being who can't actually speak is puzzling, but many clairaudient psychics, such as the famous medium Doris Stokes, now passed on, hear 'voices' very loudly and distinctly.

The use of clairaudience is probably more common than clairvoyance and most practising mediums will tell you that they hear voices, although they cannot always tell you the source. Most mediums say that their voices are nurturing and positive, rather than being destructive in any way, unlike the voices heard by schizophrenics, for example, which often tell them to do harm, either to themselves or others.

Clairaudience is most often used in psychic counselling for communication with the recently dead, in order to help those grieving on the earthly plane. A good session will leave the client far less distressed than before, and sometimes it helps just to hear that the beloved person who has passed over is thinking of them and has their interests at heart.

This kind of communication can be extremely comforting, and whether the truth is that the psychic is actually communicating with the dead or is somehow getting the information from the client at an unconscious level doesn't much matter. The proof of the pudding is in the eating and very many people have been helped by this kind of communication. Many say that the sessions helped them to have a more positive outlook on life, and to learn to live again after a bereavement rather than being devastated by the death. There is reassurance that death is not the end and that, somehow, there will be a reunion, either on another plane or through reincarnation.

However sceptical people may be, nothing which brings genuine comfort, which does not hurt anybody and which helps people to cope with everyday life should be scorned.

CLAIRVOYANCE

Many psychics call themselves 'clairvoyants'. This doesn't mean only that they are able to see ghosts or other spirits, but that they are able to see things that might be hidden from other people by using their psychic powers. A clairvoyant might be able to see what is going to happen to you over the next few months or see more clearly than you what your situation is as present.

All psychics practise clairvoyance, although the gift varies from person to person. What they see is not always accurate and in any case, the terms 'soon' or 'in the future' may be misleading. In the psychic world, 'soon' may be 25 years away or next week, so beware of a too literal interpretation.

The only way of assessing apparent clairvoyance is to ask whether it resonates with you. Many people professing clairvoyance have very little, if any, true gift.

CRYSTALS

The use of crystals is becoming ever more common in everyday life, with the proliferation of shops and mail-order firms selling various stones which can, apparently, help you to harmonize your life.

Crystal balls do not have any innate psychic power, but are used by some mediums and psychic as a kind of focus, an amplifier to aid concentration. In fact they can serve as a focus in everyday life for anyone. Many people I know who are nervous of flying hold their special crystal during the flight to calm them down. I have actually never seen a serious psychic use a crystal ball, although many of them use crystals in their original state.

In ancient times, certain crystals were believed to contain magical powers. Now this idea has been resurrected with the notion that certain mineral formations are packed with energy which can influence health and happiness. It is believed that certain crystals have links with solar energies and can aid healing.

Very many psychics now use crystals. If nothing else, they look pretty and seem 'caring'. The colours and formations are attractive, and certainly the presence of crystals in a person's home gives it a special harmonious, calm and peaceful atmosphere.

I like crystals, as they provide an aesthetic focus to the consultation, even if the evidence for their psychic energies remains controversial. I also like the kind of psychics who use crystals.

DIVINATION AND
FORTUNE-TELLING

Many people who consult psychics want to know what the future will hold. Ever since ancient times, psychics and clairvoyants have predicted future events, although very often they have not been believed.

Divination is still an important part of psychic counselling and most counsellors say they can give an indication of events that will happen six to twelve months ahead. But divination has never produced consistent results, so the most you can hope for is an indication of what is likely to happen, based on an interpretation of past events.

For instance, all psychics understand that every action has a consequence and that whatever we sow, so shall we reap. Many divinations are based on this concept and as such may be more the direct consequence of certain actions than our predetermined fate. Most modern psychics believe that we have free will, but that if we set a particular course of action in motion, there will be an inevitable consequence, eventually.

As tools of divination psychics may use tea-leaves—these are of course less popular now that tea-bags are universally used—a crystal ball, tarot cards, astrology or palmistry. The point of these, or other rituals, is that they focus the psychic's energy on the matter in hand and allow them to concentrate fully. The art of divination is one which uses intuition and imagination rather than reason or logic. All diviners have a degree of intuitive ability, some more than others.

Divination is not magic, but consists of insights based on intuition and a genuine wish to help the client. It does not seek to alter the course of events, merely to give an indication of them. Magic, by contrast, tries to alter events in the favour of the person carrying out the magic rituals, although whether it actually succeeds is open to question.

In her book *Divination*, Cherry Gilchrist make the point that the decision to practise divination is rarely arrived at on an intellectual level. Those who become diviners get 'feelings' about people and events, and may eventually decide to practise this professionally. It is very important that those who practise divination have clear, unclouded minds and emotions. In other words, they should not be going through intense traumas and emotional upheavals of their own, as these are liable to cloud the issue.

The point of a divinatory reading is that it can—or should—be able to interpret apparent random and chaotic events, and see the underlying patterns. It is this ability which gives such people insights into the future, as what happens in the future is intimately based on past and present events.

People often consult those gifted with the power of divination when they feel their own lives are in a mess. There can be no guarantee that diviners will be able to help, of course, and if you consult a fortune-teller, beware of too glib explanations or interpretations of your situation. Even the most practised diviners cannot be right all the time.

Cherry Gilchrist says that divination involves travelling beyond the limits of ordinary, rational knowledge into a realm where we can discover a different kind of knowledge.

The whole point of going for a divinatory reading, as for obtaining any other kind of psychic information, is to gain some element of control over events, to gain a sense of purpose and to stop being a victim of circumstance. Through such a reading, we learn that we set events in motion and that the consequences of these events, for good or ill, have to be played out to the end.

DOWSING

This is the term given to using a pendulum, or other device, to obtain information. Some psychics may use a pendulum to help increase the intuitive faculty.

Dowsing has been used for centuries to find water, minerals and oil, and there is no doubt that it often works. Science has not yet been able to explain why, but the tool used—pendulum, stick, divining-rod—seems to call up what is in the unconscious to conscious awareness.

Although anybody can practise dowsing, it does seem to be a gift, and one which most psychics possess.

DREAMS AND DREAMING

Dreams have always been perceived as significant and were the province of the psychic until Freud published his *Interpretation of Dreams* at the beginning of the century. Since then, dream analysis has been extensively used by orthodox psychiatrists and Freudian analysts in their work with patients.

Some, although by no means all, psychics use dream analysis and their interpretation of symbols may be quite different from that of a psychoanalyst. Even to this day, nobody really knows what dreams signify and any analysis will be at least partly a matter of guesswork.

In ancient times, dreams were considered to be prophetic, but now they are more likely to be regarded as the unconscious mind's attempt to make sense of past happenings. Psychics who use dream analysis will ask you to write down your dreams on waking. If you do this regularly, you will probably discover that they form a pattern and you will be able to work out their probable meanings for yourself.

If you are troubled by nightmares, sleep walking or halluci-nations, a visit to a psychic who specializes in dream analysis will probably help you to overcome your fears, although it must be remembered that many bad dreams these days are caused by strong medication or sleeping pills, rather than being visited by demons during the night.

Many people are troubled by recurring dreams and this is where a competent dream analyst can help. My own belief is that recurring dreams come to remind us of something as yet unresolved. As soon as we have resolved the problem, the need for the dream goes and we no longer experience it. Some people say they have 'beautiful' dreams, but it seems most likely that dreams are always symbolic indications of some kind of trouble or trauma, and that if we remember them when we wake, we should take them seriously.

Sometimes, just confronting a dream, bringing it out into the open, helps it to go away.

ECTOPLASM

In Victorian times it was common for psychics apparently to produce streams of a cloudy white substance rather like muslin from their mouths when in a trance. This was called ectoplasm. It has completely gone out of fashion and most claims about ectoplasm were found to be fraudulent when investigated. In any case, nobody ever really discovered the point of ectoplasm, and it remains a mystery.

ELEMENTALS

These are the fairies, gnomes, elves and pixies beloved of folklore. There are tales of them in every culture but so far science has failed to ratify their existence. However, they are making a comeback in some psychic circles. In the early days of the Findhorn community in Scotland, for example, fairies and other elementals were apparently seen by some people, although nowadays they appear to have all flown away.

It seems to me that elementals are rather like ghosts, auras and other phenomena unseen by most of us: thought-forms that for some people take an almost physical shape and identity. It is most likely that they don't 'exist' in any gross material sense, but are aspects of thought, intuition and clairvoyance.

If you go to see a psychic who talks of elementals, make sure the fairies he or she sees are only good ones. Avoid any psychic or medium who can, apparently, see devils and demons. Any association with 'black magic' is to be avoided.

ESP (EXTRA-SENSORY PERCEPTION)

This is the collective name given to the 'sixth sense'—the extra faculty possessed by psychics which enables them to see or predict things ignored by or hidden from other people.

EXORCISM

This is the act of getting rid of ghosts or demons, usually from a place but sometimes from a person as well. Sometimes priests with no known psychic powers will try to exorcise a ghost by sprinkling holy water and muttering a few incantations. This may work to rid a place of an apparition, but in some cases a ghost has been known to keep appearing.

Practising psychics are often called in to exorcise ghosts and they do this by neutralizing the atmosphere, visualizing it as a place of peace and harmony, rather than one troubled by earthbound spirits. With exorcism, it is probably the power of suggestion that works (or doesn't), rather than anything else.

In spite of professed widespread scepticism, most people do believe in the paranormal, in ghosts and demons, and even the most sane and rational will consider calling in a psychic if there is a bad or chilling atmosphere.

Lady Bronwen Astor, now a psychotherapist, had Stephen Ward's cottage on the Cliveden estate exorcised after his suicide in 1963. She said publicly that she had never sensed such an evil atmosphere around any place before. Ward, an osteopath, used to bring young girls—Christine Keeler and Mandy Rice-Davies are famous examples—to his cottage and practise a type of witchcraft to increase his power over people.

GHOSTS

What are exactly are ghosts and do they exist? The debate goes on. Most psychics definitely believe in their existence and the majority verdict is that ghosts are earthbound spirits who are so attached to places, or to the material plane, that they cannot leave it, but hang around annoying people.

Clearly, there is much that we don't understand, and it is just possible that some people leave such a strong presence around after they die that it becomes almost physical to the extra-sensitive.

There are too many stories of ghosts around for us to be able to dismiss them completely, but whether they have any actual material substance is unlikely. Our minds can conjure up all kinds of images, and we often believe we clearly see things which are not there, usually momentarily. Even if ghosts do exist, they are completely harmless and there is no need to be frightened of them.

GRAPHOLOGY

Graphology is the art of reading character and destiny by analysing handwriting. I believe graphology can be extremely accurate and it is now used extensively for recruitment in the business world, especially in America. As with any other psychic gift, accuracy with graphology depends partly on intuition and very much on practice and application.

Of course, like anything else, there are good graphologists and mediocre ones. The best ones are astonishingly accurate, while the others are best avoided. Some psychologists frown on graphology, saying that handwriting depends on the country we were born in—you can tell an American and a French hand instantly—on our level of artistic ability and depth of education. Maybe—but those things are all 'us'. No two people have identical handwriting.

I'm afraid I judge people very much on their handwriting, especially their signatures, as I believe handwriting is a very plain and easy guide to character, aspirations, hopes, fears, self-confidence, ego and the state of mental, physical and emotional health. You can't easily hide or disguise your handwriting, and even if you try, a competent graphologist will be able to find you out.

HYPNOSIS

Some psychics use hypnosis, although most don't. But don't be surprised if, during a counselling session, you go into a state of altered consciousness. Many people are nervous of going to see a psychic because they are afraid of being hypnotized against their will. In fact, this is extremely unlikely to happen, and although most psychics will do their best to help you to relax, they will not actually put you under.

Hypnotherapy, these days, is used more by non-psychics to help people with problems like smoking, phobias and child abuse, than for actual psychic guidance.

I CHING

The *I Ching* is a highly complicated Chinese system of attempting to make sense of the universe, a book of hexagrams used as a form of divination. The idea is that everything that exists is a combination of masculine and feminine forces, yin and yang. The *I Ching* appeals to those who like numbers, boxes and some kind of mathematical order. It is becoming ever more popular with Western psychics, but takes years to understand and use properly.

If you go to see a psychic who uses the *I Ching* for divination, you do not need to understand it yourself, although some people find it fun. In order to appreciate it fully, you need to have the kind of mind that enjoys solving crossword puzzles and playing chess, I feel.

KARMA

This is a word you are very likely nowadays to hear a psychic using. It is Sanskrit for 'action' and means, simply, that every action has a consequence. In Christian terms, it is expressed in 'as you sow, so shall you reap.

Most psychics these days believe in reincarnation, although there are many different theories as to how it works. Traditional reincarnation theory believes that we do not die with the physical body, but that our souls, spirits or essences live on to inhabit other bodies. We incarnate in order to learn important lessons. Lessons will be repeated until we get the message, when they will stop.

Professor Ian Stevenson, of the University of Virginia, has interviewed literally thousands of children who appear to remember past lives—and come to the conclusion that for very many, there is an X-factor which defies all rational and scientific explanation.

There is as yet no conclusive proof that would satisfy a sceptic. Increasingly, though, practising psychics ask their clients to take on board reincarnation as if it were a fact and proceed from there.

KIRLIAN PHOTOGRAPHY

This is a method of photography invented in Russia during the 1930s which is supposedly able to photograph the aura around living things—people, animals and plants. Although it has been around for so long, it has never quite gained respectability and my own feeling is that it is falling into disuse. In any case, it may be that the method of photography simply records an electrical charge around living matter, rather than anything more mysterious.

Kirlian photography has its adherents, but it's easy for both client and psychic to deceive themselves about the apparent meaning behind the fuzzy lines of the Kirlian images.

LEVITATION

As a journalist on a mass-market tabloid in the 1970s, from time to time I had to go and investigate claims of levitation. Never once did anybody levitate in my presence—although of course this does not mean that it is impossible!

Claims of levitation were popular in the nineteenth century, the golden age of psychic investigation, but almost all were discovered to be fraudulent.

More recently, adherents of Transcendental Meditation have claimed to be able to levitate. In fact, this is simply hopping on sprung mattresses in the lotus position, something anybody practised in yoga can do. It is not possible for people to levitate—we are not aerodynamically sound enough—and any claims by psychics that they are able to levitate should be dismissed. In any case, what would be the point of it?

MEDITATION

Most, if not all, practising psychics these days place great emphasis on meditation. This increases the psychic faculty as it helps intuition and clear sight to be developed. In order to be able to help clients, psychics need to recharge their batteries, empty their minds of extraneous and negative matter, and keep their heads clear. Meditation means getting into the alpha mode, and brings about harmony between the left and right sides of the brain.

There has been a certain amount of scientific research into meditation, and there seems little doubt that insights and flashes of intuition can arise from this ability to look inwards. Meditation, works on the assumption that, at some level of our being, we know all that we need to know. We actually contain within ourselves wisdom, power, love, insights and healing ability (meditation is now increasingly accepted as an effective method of healing). The trouble is that most of us lead such frenetic lives that we never learn to listen to that 'still small voice' and we have forgotten how to trust it.

For most of us, meditation does not come naturally and has to be learned. Sitting in silence can, at first, be an extremely painful and disconcerting experience, as all kinds of unwelcome thoughts may rise up, and there is a wish to damp them down again. Meditation can also be extremely boring.

But those who have mastered the art say that, during these moments of stillness and silence, when everything external is blotted out, comes truth and increased awareness of how things are, or how they could be. Many creative people have found that they must retreat into silence from time to time in order to tap the creative impulse.

Some psychics use guided meditation to help their clients relax and feel at ease. For this, they may play a tape or use soothing words and make suggestions as to helpful patterns of thinking during meditation.

NUMEROLOGY

Numerology works rather like a horoscope, in that you have to give your date of birth, your full name and a few other details to the numerologist who will then add them up and jostle them around to get a reading of your character and destiny.

If you like and are adept with numbers, this form of psychic consultation may work for you, and many people I know swear by it, but I have never had much success with it, possibly because I am horribly innumerate and find character reading or divination by use of numbers boring and tedious. But since ancient times, numbers and sequences of numbers have been considered to have their own magic, and many people find them fascinating. In fact numerology is increasing in popularity.

OUIJA BOARD

A ouija board is a board used to conjure up spirits and communicate with them (the word comes from the French and German for yes). At one time used extensively by spiritualists to speak to those 'on the other side', it is less frequently employed as a psychic aid nowadays.

You used to be able to buy commercial ouija boards, but now they have been outlawed world-wide as they have been known to terrify people who have used them at amateur seances. But there is nothing to stop people from making letters, putting them in a circle, and then all touching a glass or other object to see whether there is anybody there. Use of a ouija board should not be undertaken lightly, however, and a practised psychic should always be present.

I have never been to a professional psychic or medium who uses a ouija board, but no doubt one can come across them. I personally do find them rather frightening, although it's hard to say exactly why—possibly because of their association with old-time horror movies and folklore.

OUT-OF-THE-BODY EXPERIENCES

An out-of-the-body experience (OBE) happens when you appear to leave your body and float in space while your actual body is sitting or lying down obeying as usual the laws of gravity. OBEs are alarming when they first happen, but researchers estimate that as many as one in ten people have had such an experience. In near-death experiences (NDEs), now more common with the advent of life-support machines, patients also commonly report a sensation of being out of their bodies, floating on the ceiling, and travelling to a place which is all lightness and peace.

Sometimes, during an OBE, people try to do something practical, switch on a light, for instance, only to find their fingers move right through the switch and nothing happens. OBEs can happen as the result of taking certain drugs, such as hash or LSD, although such experiences are not guaranteed through use of these substances.

Out-of-the-body experiences have been extensively investigated in recent years, along with near-death experiences. Some researchers believe there is nothing paranormal or mystical about OBEs and NDEs, and that eventually all will be explained in terms of neurology. The consensus of opinion, however, is that the increasing frequency of OBEs and NDEs indicates that there is, at least, 'something' beyond the physical, although quite what that is has not yet been conclusively determined.

It is common for people's perceptions of themselves and the world to be altered dramatically after an OBE. For some people, it validates a belief in astral bodies, life after life and the spiritual dimension. At the very least, it frequently motivates people to become serious investigators of the paranormal.

PALMISTRY

Palmistry is a highly complicated art—or science—and one which seems to be making something of a comeback. Many aspects of the hands are noted in a palm reading, and, as with astrology or numerology, correct interpretation takes a lot of practice and hard work. It is not a party game for the amateur. I believe that if the psychic is gifted enough, palmistry can be as accurate as graphology. It seems to me entirely logical that character, aspirations, tendencies and so on can be divined from reading a palm, as hands are so very individual and vary so much from person to person. Not only are no two hands alike, but the left hand will also be quite different from the right.

Palmists work quite differently from each other. Some will give your hands a fairly cursory glance while others will measure the lines very carefully with mathematical instruments. Recent work on palmistry has indicated that hands can be a potent indicator of states of health, both mental and physical.

You can now buy books on reading palms for children, but this should not be taken to mean that palmistry is not a serious art. It has been practised for centuries, and can give highly accurate results.

Palmists say they can tell from the hand whether a person is intelligent, whether they work mainly with their hands or with their brain, and whether they are energetic or idle. Fingers which bend back easily are supposed to indicate a flexible, versatile, open mind, whereas full flexibility indicates a brilliant mind.

Palmistry readings are highly detailed, and the palmist will look not only at the lines on your hand, but how long the fingers are, whether there is a wide gap between the fingers, whether they are thick or thin, whether the palm is skinny and narrow or wide and flat, and whether or not it is hollow. The fineness or coarseness of the skin will yield valuable information, as will the softness or hardness of the hands under pressure.

Through reading hands, palmists can tell whether the client is sensual or intellectual, whether he or she is vulgar and showy or quiet and refined, and also the attitude towards money.

As with other aspects of psychic counselling, intuition and long practice inform this art. There is no clinical scientific data on palmistry as there is with astrology, but it is an art which has been used for thousands of years, and there is general agreement among practitioners as to the character and inclinations indicated by certain types of hand. Most reputable psychics will refuse to read the hands of children, as the lines change so much.

PAST-LIFE THERAPY

Past-life or regression therapy is said to help solve problems in this life, such as phobias and unaccountable fears. The rationale behind this is that very often people have problems which seem unrelated to any event in their present existence and an examination of their past lives may bring forth explanations and then recovery. For example, most people who fear flying have never been involved in a plane crash, nor have any of their relatives. Regression may show that they were, for instance, fighter pilots during World War Two who were shot down in flames. Likewise, a morbid fear of water might be related to death by drowning in a past life.

This form of therapy is becoming highly popular now, but has to be practised by somebody who knows exactly what they are doing, as it may involve quite deep hypnosis. I feel that past-life therapy is not something to be embarked on lightly, and certainly not just for fun, even though it *is* fun to get a glimpse of what your past lives might have been. The trouble is, there is usually no way of checking them out, no way of knowing whether you really did live that life or whether you are dimly remembering a film or book.

Past-life therapy can certainly often help people to put their present lives into perspective, but my feeling is that it should be reserved for trying to solve serious problems, rather than for idle curiosity, simply because you don't know what might come up, or how you might react. Sometimes there is a strong emotional reaction but at others 'remembering' an apparent past life is simply like watching an item on the television which hardly engages you.

I have had several sessions of past-life therapy and would say that although I have no idea whether I recalled real past lives or half-remembered bits of history books and novels, I had the very strong feeling that I could not lie or make up a more interesting life to please the therapist. What came up seemed to do so of its own accord and I could not control it.

Nowadays, several medically-trained psychiatrists and Jungian analysts are practising past-life therapy as they feel it can be a quicker and more effective way than traditional analysis to help their patients. But also, all kinds of untrained people are now offering this and I feel one has to be careful.

POLTERGEISTS

These so-called 'noisy ghosts' are almost always conjured up by teenagers, often from highly disturbed backgrounds. It seems that in some way poltergeist activity is generated by the teenager, rather than there being any outside ghost, although a convincing explanation of why pools of water appear, objects fly around the room and electrical gadgets switch themselves on has never been found.

Poltergeist activity seems quite rare and youngsters usually grow out of it. It most commonly occurs at around the time of puberty—for girls near their first menstruation and for boys when the growth spurt starts. The most famous teenager to be surrounded by poltergeist activity was Matthew Manning, now a respected and highly successful healer. Matthew as a teenager was amazingly psychic, and his experiences at boarding school—which must have amazed and delighted his fellow pupils—have been written up in his fascinating book *The Link*. Matthew was in touch with long-dead people, and used to practise automatic writing and automatic art. His faculties have been extensively researched, and there seems no doubt that he can affect matter in a highly mysterious way which does not obey known scientific laws.

PSI

This Greek word has now almost completely replaced the term 'extra-sensory perception', but means much the same thing. Psi is used mainly by professional parapsychologists, and covers every aspect of psychic phenomena including telepathy, clairvoyance, precognition, psychokinesis and psychometry.

PSYCHIC SELF-DEFENCE

All serious psychics practise psychic self-defence, which means they must know when to open up and close down the psychic faculty, and how to protect themselves against negative or harmful influences.

Psychics are, above all, extremely open to impressions, atmospheres and other people's states of mind. They are like a sponge, absorbing everything into themselves, and they must know how to squeeze themselves out and keep dry when necessary. This is done mainly by visualization, imagining the psychic centres opening up and closing at will.

Some psychics protect themselves by putting on an invisible dark cloak with a hood before they go out and seeing themselves being safeguarded by this.

PSYCHIC SURGERY

Psychic surgery, a branch of spiritual healing, is surgery performed on the aura using invisible instruments. A psychic surgeon operates on the 'etheric body' which is about 12 inches away from the physical one.

Although it sounds peculiar in the extreme, one or two practitioners have had incredible success using psychic surgery. It came to prominence when certain Filipino peasants were supposed to be able to perform this feat. Although some were undoubtedly fraudulent, not all claims could be easily dismissed. The magician James Randi has demonstrated on television how apparent psychic surgery can be mere sleight of hand, although why anybody should want to do this remains a mystery.

Psychic surgery is not very widely practised, however, and I would advise going to a psychic surgeon only on the strongest recommendation, never by replying to an advertisement.

PSYCHOKINESIS

The name given to metal-bending, or the apparent ability to change the molecular structure of metal or other dense objects. Although many people are extremely sceptical of this ability, laboratory experiments have shown that some people can indeed bend metal simply by stroking it. There may be a large amount of cheating going on, but some experiments have been too carefully controlled for this to be a possibility.

Most psychics do not possess this ability or, if they do, they don't make use of it. It has little if any use in psychic counselling and only serves to show that mind indeed can prevail over matter in certain circumstances. It seems to be the case that people—often youngsters—who can bend metal are psychic, and many come from disturbed backgrounds.

PSYCHOMETRY

Very frequently used in psychic consultations, psychometry is the ability to hold something in your hand, such as a ring, bracelet or other intimate object, and sense its history or importance to its owner. Some psychic consultants may ask if they can hold some precious object of yours in their hand to enable them to tune into your vibrations. There is nothing sinister about this, and it is standard psychic practice. The belief is that inanimate objects contain some energy belonging to the owner and that the psychically gifted can divine what this is.

Not all psychic counsellors use psychometry to tune into clients, but it can be a useful way in.

PYRAMID POWER

Pyramids are increasingly used for healing purposes, with people sitting in vast plastic shapes. The pyramid shape is supposed to contain a lot of power and energy and eliminate negative feelings. Pyramids are also supposed to be able to keep razor blades sharp.

RUNES

Runes are a very ancient form of divination, and consist of small stone, wood or ceramic objects carved or engraved with hieroglyphics which have special meanings. Runes are a psychic tool increasingly used these days as their power is being rediscovered. The letters or inscriptions are supposed to carry particular power and energy, and they can be used for healing, concentration or amplifying psychic powers and insights.

SEANCES

Seances are group sittings whereby the people present try to conjure up spirits of the dead. At certain times, they have been extremely popular as a kind of parlour game, but they can be extremely frightening when nobody knows what they are doing. In any group, there is likely to be some highly suggestive person who will become terrified by the proceedings, so all seances should be supervised by a trained medium who knows what they are doing, and can calm down fears and reassure people.

Some people do attend or give seances because they enjoy the sensation of being frightened, rather like watching a horror movie or video, but they can be used for serious purposes as well. The problem is, the whole business of seances has been so devalued by B-movies and amateur sessions that it has become difficult to take them seriously nowadays. Yet modern seances led by a practising medium are quite different from the popular image of a group sitting round a table in a darkened room while gradually a spirit manifests. They are much more likely to take place in an ordinary living-room, with people sitting round in chairs.

There is no doubt that powerful energies can be present when everybody is concentrating on the same thing, but whether actual spirits of the dead can enter a room by this type of concentration remains open to question.

SPIRIT GUIDES

These are the entities supposedly existing in the spirit world who guide and give information to certain mediums. Sometimes mediums will go into a trance, an altered state of consciousness, in order to contact the guide, and sometimes the guide will 'come through' when the medium is sitting in an apparently ordinary state. Some mediums appear to be 'taken over' by their spirit guides and talk in a gruff whisper quite different from their ordinary speaking voice. Sometimes their personalities appear to change as well.

Nobody really knows whether spirit guides actually exist, whether they are manifestations of the medium's unconscious, whether they are aspects of vibrations coming from the client, or whether the medium is contacting their own higher self or an aspect of themselves from a previous life. Whatever the explanation, the information coming from a spirit guide will, if the medium is genuine, be positive and helpful.

Mediums believe they are simply acting as channels for the information and that they have to work hard to make sure the channel remains clear. Therefore, they will not usually drink alcohol, they will be careful of their diet and will abstain from sex before embarking on a session, simply so that the channel does not become muddied. In some cases, quite startling information can come apparently from a spirit guide.

TAROT

Tarot cards, once considered extremely mysterious and possibly devilish and occult, are now becoming increasingly used, to the point where 'tarot lines' have been set up in tabloid newspapers. These may be fun, but are unlikely to be of much use to the individual as, like newspaper stars, they are far too generalized.

In essence, the tarot pack, used since antiquity for divining and fortune-telling, is another way of amplifying information which comes from paranormal, or extra-sensory, sources. Most practitioners of tarot believe that these ancient cards offer an opportunity for self-knowledge, to clarify the past, present and future, and to put us more in control of our fate. As with astrology and palmistry, each person's tarot reading will be different. It is something which should be used for individual readings, and as such, should be treated seriously.

The cards, 78 in all, are divided into the major arcana of 22 cards and the minor arcana of 56 cards. It is the major arcana which is supposed to provide the main insights into our destiny and character. The minor arcana corresponds roughly to our modern pack of playing cards with four suits: cups, swords, pentacles and sceptres. There are 14 cards in each suit.

If you go to half a dozen psychics all using tarot cards, you will find they each use them in a completely individual way. There is no set way of using or interpreting the tarot, and the accuracy or otherwise of the reading depends on the skill and intuitive faculties of the clairvoyant.

Although tarot cards are supposed to have magical qualities, they are nothing to worry about. It must be said, though, that most psychics who use the tarot imbue them with mystical significance and may keep them carefully wrapped in silk or cloth, in a special place. They are always laid out in a special way, and people who use them develop their own favourite ways of shuffling and laying out the cards. But just because they have recently become popular, this does not mean they have any greater inherent powers than crystals, pendulums or other psychic amplifiers.

Tarot cards have been read in the same way for at least 500 years, and interpretations do not vary significantly. Edwin J. Nigg, author of *Revealing the Secrets of the Tarot*, believes that this should give confidence in a tarot reading, even if the mechanism by which the cards work has never been fully understood.

The tarot cards, like other methods of divination, do not exactly foretell the future, but they can help us to think about our past, to analyse our present situation and to use these insights to think clearly about the future. They should not be used with people who are mentally ill or who have serious psychiatric or personality problems, and most psychics using tarot emphasize that they should be used only for serious problems, and then only for one specific problem at a time, such as a relationship or job difficulty, clarity on whether to move location or on the outcome of an illness.

Basically, tarot offers a means by which genuine seekers can gain clarity and a sense of purpose in their lives. It is best to go on a personal recommendation when consulting a tarot reader, as anybody can buy a pack of cards and set up as a counsellor.

TELEPATHY

As we have already seen, this is the name given to the ability to communicate thoughts, and possibly feelings, from one mind to another without anything being said.

Most non-psychics gain telepathic insights only with those they know well. There seems to be a very strong telepathic link between mothers and their small children, but this does not extend to all women and all small children. Psychically gifted people, however, can 'read' the minds of people they don't know well by tapping into their vibrations, energies, auras, or what you will.

For instance, I once went to a psychic for help with a difficult decision. I had been offered a very nice job which involved working with somebody whom I had been extremely close to many years before. Then neither of us had been single and free, but now the situation had changed. I wondered whether this person wanted more from me than a working relationship, and whether he was hoping that he might be able to live with me and have an intimate relationship.

The psychic I consulted 'tuned in' to the vibrations and said, 'No, I don't think that's in his mind at all. He is somebody who is more like a father to you, and also, in some ways, a son. He respects the work that you do, and values it highly. He doesn't have in mind any other type of relationship other than that of close working colleagues.'

This was a load off my mind, but also—it was true. Immediately, I felt more confident and that if I decided to take the job, the relationship would be easy and without strings or intimate attachments.

Telepathy is a useful ability, and even people who do not have marked psychic gifts can enlarge their telepathic abilities by trying to forget about themselves and tap into how another person feels, what they are thinking, what vibrations they are putting out.

VOODOO

The word 'voodoo' is African, and is usually used to describe a system of magic which was brought by slaves to Haiti, where it took root. Basically, voodoo involves wild dancing to whip up a state of altered consciousness or frenzy, so that 'spirits' can take over the bodies of ordinary men and women. They become possessed and thus able to perform acts of magic which in their ordinary state would be impossible.

Voodoo has always been held in fear and fascination. It has long been associated with black magic and witchcraft, and has come to mean putting a curse on somebody, wishing them ill. The popular image of a voodoo ritual—the subject of hundreds of horror films—is making a doll and sticking pins into it, whereupon the person represented by the doll, who may be miles or even countries away, gives a scream of horror and drops down dead or writhes in terrible agony.

No reputable psychic counsellor, however, would ever use voodoo rituals or put curses on people. Counsellors are there to help.

The next chapter will review whether this form of therapy is for you.

FOUR

IS IT FOR YOU?

You now know what psychic counselling is about. But how do you decide whether it might be for you? I think possibly the first question to ask is: can my particular problem, whatever it is, be dealt with in any other way? In other words, is a psychic counsellor the very best person to help me in this particular instance? Sometimes just talking to a friend or listening to the dictates of your heart will give you the answers just as effectively. And no psychic has *all* the answers.

As with any therapist, it's important to avoid dependence, to imagine that 'looking into the crystal ball' gives magical solutions to every problem. We have all heard of people who feel they can't move without consulting their psychic or laying out a spread of tarot cards. The idea of seeing a psychic is often appealing, because many of them have an exotic box of tricks at their fingertips, and it sounds exciting to have an aura reading or to sit inside a plastic pyramid.

The sensible course lies between imagining that because psychic matters sound strange they must all be rubbish and believing psychics and clairvoyants are so much the fount of all wisdom that you can't set out on any course of action without going to see your pet medium. People professing psychic powers should be viewed in the same way as any other advice givers: sometimes useful, and there when you need them, but not to be depended on for everything.

Although some psychics are enormously intuitive and have learned great wisdom from tapping into and trusting that aspect of themselves, all—like the rest of us—are flawed humans, all are liable to have off days, and all may give wrong advice or get hold of the wrong end of the stick. There is no psychic in the world who sees everything clearly all the time. To do that, you would have to be God. No human being gets it right all the time. One of the problems with psychics, though, especially male ones, is that they can sometimes come to believe that they are more powerful than they really are, especially if they are charismatic enough to attract adoring clients. Although psychics and clairvoyants can give useful perspectives, they can only put forward suggestions and possibilities. Always beware of suspending your judgement and relying too greatly on what comes out of a session.

Having said that, there may be times when nobody but a really experienced psychic can help you.

When considering whether psychic counselling might be for you, there are several things to bear in mind. There should be a strong wish to gain something of value from the encounter. You should not go either in a spirit of scepticism or imagining that all your problems will be instantly solved. You could wish to gain some clarity or insight, or be seeking comfort or reassurance. Maybe you are interested in communicating with a person who is no longer in the physical body. Perhaps you would like to gain important information about your job or personal relationships.

Whatever the presenting factor, it seems to me that seeking psychic help should be reserved for serious life events. Its power is, or can be, too great for trivialities. Because even if you go to see somebody with psychic powers for 'fun', you may be disturbed at how deep your feelings and reactions are. This may happen whether you believe their psychic powers are an external reality or whether you think it's all the power of suggestion and that there is nothing of any greater significance in the work they do.

There can, of course, be no absolute guarantee that a visit to a psychic will help you, any more than a doctor can be guaranteed to cure your complaint. But at the very least true

psychics, those with genuine powers, should be able to enable
you gain insights about yourself and those around you, and
impart hope for the future by enabling you to view things in a
wider perspective.

Although you may like to see a psychic for general direction,
there are certain specific times when a psychic might be able to
offer the kind of help not easily available from another source.
These are:

bereavement;

when you have a strong feeling that you've lived before
and want to try to get to the bottom of it;

you, or somebody close to you, has had experiences
which appear to be of a psychic nature—you get
premonitions, you feel you have seen a ghost or you've
had an out-of-the-body experience and would like to
make sense of it all;

you hear voices and have been told you are schizophrenic
or need to see a psychiatrist;

your child has an imaginary friend;

you want to know why you engage in behavioural
patterns which are self-destructive;

you feel you are at a crossroads in your life and don't
know which way to turn.

We'll deal with these in turn.

BEREAVEMENT

This is possibly the commonest reason of all for visiting a
psychic. When faced with a sudden and devastating bereavement, even the most cynical and sceptical can find it difficult to
believe that death is indeed the end and that they will never

see or have contact with the beloved person again.

Sometimes, the bereaved person may simply want evidence of survival, some reassurance that physical death is *not* the end, as they may previously have believed. More often, though, they are desperate to make contact the dead person, to try and alleviate, in some measure, the sense of terrible loss they feel.

In a society that worships everything to do with the body and material things, the decay and eventual destruction of the body is hard to accept. Such is our fear of death that we do not want to admit it exists, that we are not going to last on this earthly plane forever. This may be why ever more people are visiting psychics to gain some kind of evidence of survival.

At most spiritualist churches, the clairvoyant will ask the people present whether there is anybody they want to make contact with and indeed, this is a major reason for people going to spiritualist services. Those who have been happily married hope to be reunited, and those who have lost children or other close relatives want to hear from them again, even though not in bodily form.

Sessions of psychic counselling do not necessarily take away all the grief, or the need to mourn, but they can help you turn your attention towards the positive rather than focusing on the negative. In particular, seeing a psychic when upset by a sudden loss can alleviate self-pity—the main emotion experienced when somebody close dies.

If they are not unhappy, the psychic will ask you to consider why should you be?

Carol, a beauty therapist, was devastated when a former lover, Stan, was suddenly killed in a car crash at the age of 48. Although the relationship had been a platonic one for very many years and he had married somebody else several years previously, they had kept in close contact. Carol was surprised that as the months went by, she could not seem to get over his death.

She said:

I could have understood it if I'd been married to him or if a close relative had suddenly died. But because our relationship had been a fairly casual one for so many years, I was surprised that I kept thinking about him and bursting into tears at work.

In the end, I felt I had to have some kind of help and a friend suggested going to see a psychic at the College of Psychic Studies. I had never in my life visited a psychic and had never even been interested in anything like that. But somehow I felt I had to make contact with my friend. I felt that there was some unfinished business between us, something I suppose I had hoped to sort out before he died and now it was too late. I had this overwhelming feeling that it was all too late, that I had missed my chance to tell him how fond I was of him and how often he was in my thoughts. It was as if a part of me had been snatched away and as if the relationship had suddenly ended without ever being satisfactorily resolved.

I was very nervous when I went to see the psychic because I had no idea at all what might happen. The person I saw was an elderly man who had been strongly recommended to me. Instantly, he put me at my ease and he didn't do anything weird, like going into a trance, which I felt might make me flip completely.

But it was all very ordinary, and matter of fact. I sat in one chair and he sat opposite me. Eventually, he started to talk and it was as if Stan was speaking directly to me. The psychic told me things that he could never have known and I had a very strong feeling that Stan was in the room.

Because Stan had a very difficult marriage and had left his wife some time before he died, I think I imagined that we might get together again and that was why I was so very upset about his death. Stan explained that, so far as he was concerned, we'd had a relationship, that it was at an end but that he would always be very fond of me and that he would be there in the spirit world for me. We weren't meant to have an ongoing relationship in this world.

I don't know what I made of it, whether it was really Stan speaking or whether the psychic was making it up. Obviously, I have no real way of knowing. But through the psychic—I had six sessions in all—we went through every aspect of our relationship together and at the end I felt satisfied. I knew then why it would never have worked out on a long-term basis, and I felt stronger and more able to cope than I had done in the past.

Without really realizing it, I had been mourning the loss of Stan for many years and that was why I had never been able to form a proper relationship with anybody else. But having psychic counselling enabled me to put it into perspective, and answered some questions about myself and my own life.

I'd been experiencing severe difficulties at work, but through the psychic, Stan gave me some advice about what to do about setting up on my own, which I have now done. I'm not saying everything is plain sailing, but the contact enabled me to do two things: finally release Stan from my thoughts, and find the courage to set up my own business rather than working for somebody else.

I now feel that Stan is with me. Even if it was all the power of suggestion, and even if it was wishful thinking on my part that I really did make contact, I can't deny the difference it has made to my life. I am no longer afraid of death, and I feel a kind of calmness and peace about my life which I never felt before. I was still longing for my past lover, but that longing has now gone, and I have achieved a new kind of self-confidence.

For me, psychic counselling was the only answer and I certainly felt that the medium I went to see was absolutely genuine. He seemed only to want to help.

PAST LIVES

It seems to be these days that ever more people are having the feeling that they've lived before, that this physical body is not all. Perhaps more of us are receiving memories of past lives or maybe we are all becoming more open to the possibility.

Whatever the explanation, past-life counselling is becoming more and more popular. These days, most psychics and clairvoyants completely accept reincarnation, although there is a wide variety of opinion as to exactly how it works. Some people believe we reincarnate instantly, others that we may remain on the astral plane for many, possibly hundreds of years. There is a school of opinion which believes we may split off after physical death and enter into a number of different bodies, hence the ever-growing population, and another which believes only some people reincarnate.

Some psychics adhere to the idea that we get better with each new incarnation, as we keep learning important lessons; others, that we get ever more vicious and impure with each bodily form we take on. Nobody knows for sure, as there is no way of checking it out, but most people who have studied the paranormal for any length of time eventually come to believe in some kind of reincarnation, even if they would hesitate to say exactly how it works.

Finding out about the possibility of a past life is another important reason for going to see a clairvoyant.

Estelle could not make sense of life when her daughter was born severely physically and mentally handicapped. She kept asking herself, 'Why me, why Emma?' None of the doctors in hospital, counsellors or religious advisors she contacted could help her in any way, or give her any good reasons as to why it might have happened.

All Estelle knew was that she felt desperately guilty and ashamed, and could not feel 'right' about anything after it had happened. She, like most mothers these days, had fully expected to give birth to a perfectly normal child and there were no indications from such prenatal tests as were available when Estelle was pregnant that anything could be wrong.

When Emma was 14, it became clear that she would have to go and live in a home. Although she might live to a good age, she needed round the clock nursing of a kind that would simply not be available on a home basis. It was when Emma was admitted to the home that Estelle finally felt she could not bear it, and had to at least try and discover the reason why Emma should not have been born normal, like her other two children.

Estelle said:

The religious people kept saying that it was God's will and the doctors said these things happen. They assured me there was nothing I could have done which would have prevented Emma's handicap and nothing that anybody in the hospital could have done either.

I felt strongly that it was my duty to look after her and keep her at home, but eventually she got beyond that, and there was no alternative but for her to go into care. I knew nothing more could be done at home and I was just wearing myself out trying to manage Emma. My other two children were resentful that Emma took up so much time, when she was such a nuisance. I wasn't even sure that I loved her any more.

But I kept feeling guilty, that I was to blame, or at least that somebody was to blame. I just couldn't accept Emma's handicap and I kept thinking that somehow she would grow out of it, even though I knew she wouldn't, and even when she had to go into the home.

In the end, a friend who was staying with me asked if I had ever considered psychic counselling. I hadn't, and in fact, nothing could have been further from my mind. But I thought I had nothing to lose and if anything at all could cast light on the reason for Emma's handicap, then I would consider it.

I had many sessions with the psychic before I even began to understand what she was saying. She told me that, for some reason, Emma had to incarnate into this kind of body. She had chosen to be handicapped in order to learn important lessons and she had chosen me as her mother because we had some karma to work out together.

At first, it didn't make any sense at all, but eventually it helped me to have a better attitude, to be more compassionate towards myself and to understand that Emma had her own reasons for coming to earth in such a deformed body.

I realized that there was no point in feeling guilty, that it was putting an unnecessary burden on both me and Emma. My many sessions with the psychic—I suppose I had about 15 altogether—helped me to be more compassionate towards myself and towards Emma, who I felt in some ways had blighted my life. I realized I'd always had a very ambivalent attitude towards her, although always fiercely denying this, even to myself, and talking it through with a psychic helped me to admit my true feelings.

I can't explain how reincarnation works, and many of my friends and acquaintances think I'm ridiculous when I talk to them about karma and how Emma had to incarnate in a deformed body. I've learned to keep quiet about it, and I can't expect that doctors and medical people will understand.

But what I've been helped to realize is that Emma's life isn't pointless. She had to show me something— something of love, perhaps—and she had to learn what life was like trapped in a hopeless body. To understand this at any rate is better than to keep wailing and wringing my hands and asking pointlessly, 'Why me? Why Emma? Why us?'

Why not, I've learned. Nobody is immune from the possibility of these things happening, none of us lead charmed lives where everything will automatically go right. But these days, we so expect everything to go our way that we can't handle it when life throws up such challenges.

Emma has been such a challenge, and one I've had to learn to meet. Through my sessions with a psychic, I think I've learned to be equal to the challenge. It's made me stronger, more self-resilient, less of a victim of remorseless events.

MAKING SENSE OF PSYCHIC EXPERIENCES

If you strongly feel that you are having, or have had, psychic experiences, another psychic is very often the *only* person who can help you in this matter. Other people may tell you that you are deluded or misinformed, or believe you are talking rubbish. They are unlikely to be able to make sense of the situation.

But a psychic will take you gently through the experiences you have had, reassure you that there is nothing to be afraid of, that you just have an extra sensitivity, and will help you to come to terms with the occurrences so that you can face up to them and incorporate them into the sum of your experiences.

Bernard, a business executive, was used to staying in hotels. His work took him all over the world and he attended many international conferences. At 45, he was confident, successful and high-earning. He was not in the slightest bit interested in psychic matters and if he ever gave them a thought, he dismissed them as at best harmless fun and at worst self-delusion.

However, one week he was staying in a famous five-star hotel for a week-long conference. He'd stayed in this hotel many times before. He went to bed one evening and during the night distinctly heard a baby crying. In the morning, he mentioned it to the manager who said there were no babies or children at all in the hotel.

The next night, it was the same story—a baby crying. The following night, Bernard thought he actually saw a small baby in his room. He felt very frightened and decided to make some enquiries. He discovered that about 50 years ago, a baby had died in the room where he was sleeping.

'Why should I be afraid of a long-dead baby?' he asked himself, as he went to bed the next night. But again, he heard the crying and thought he actually saw a baby. In the morning, Bernard asked the manager if he could change his room and this was arranged. The person who took over Bernard's room heard nothing.

The experience troubled Bernard, and when he returned home from the conference, he secretly contacted the Society for Psychical Research, who put him in touch with a psychic who had studied ghosts for very many years.

Bernard said:

It took a long time for my scepticism to turn into belief, but through talking to the psychic, I came to understand that perhaps I too was psychic. I distinctly heard that baby, although nobody else had, not even the person who swapped rooms with me. The psychic I went to see was very down-to-earth, an academic psychologist who had made a serious study of paranormal phenomena.

He said that the most usual explanation for ghosts was that they were earthbound spirits who for some reason were so attached to places that they were unable to ascend to another plane of existence. Some people could see them, he said, while others couldn't—but if you saw them, this meant you were extra sensitive and had psychic gifts.

To me, there was no doubt that I had both heard and seen the baby. It couldn't have been suggestion, as at the time I had no idea that an actual baby had died in that room. The experience decided me to research the matter for myself and I now have an appreciation of another dimension in my life.

I learned that I too had psychic powers and that, without being fully aware of this, had used them in my business career. For me, going to a psychic stopped me being afraid of ghosts and now I've learned that if I can see things other people can't, I can make conscious use of and harness that power rather than being nervous of it and denying it.

YOU HEAR VOICES

It is quite common—nobody knows perhaps how common—for people to hear voices telling them what to do. The most famous example in history is of course Joan of Arc, but Florence Nightingale also heard voices which propelled her to a course of action which horrified her rich and leisured family. Nearer our own times, Eileen Caddy, the co-founder of Findhorn community in Scotland, became convinced that God was speaking directly to her. Even now, Eileen always obeys the commands and advice she hears 'in guidance'.

When people hear voices, they always feel a compulsion to obey them. Some people seem to hear voices and understand immediately that they are psychic, that they have perhaps been specially called to do some great or unusual work. More often, though, hearing voices worries people, as they fear they are not quite normal and wonder if they are going round the bend.

Paula started hearing voices when she was a teenager. She had come from a very troubled alcoholic background and felt that she had to keep the secret of her parents' drinking. She grew up in America and as a teenager, her voices told her to go to England to study and get away from her family. She obeyed them, thinking that as soon as she left for another country, the voices would stop. But she kept on hearing them and eventually went to a psychiatrist for help.

His view was that I was seriously disturbed, and I spent the next few years in and out of psychiatric hospitals, where I was treated for all kinds of mental disturbance. None of it did any good and eventually I felt I had to find some other explanation, so I booked up a session with a very famous psychic.

She told me that the 'voices' I was hearing weren't a sign of being round the bend, as they constituted 'guidance'. It's when people hear voices telling them to do wicked or negative things that they may be in need of psychiatric help.

The psychic I visited reassured me that the voices meant no harm and that in fact I was lucky to hear them, as they were on my side. I had been brought up in a very rational, secular family and it was hard for me to accept that there might be something paranormal about the voices.

Gradually, through talking to the psychic and also attending mediumship circles, I gained confidence in going with the voices. I've never told my family in America about them, as they would be certain I was round the bend, but I feel now that it probably is people who come from disturbed or uncomfortable backgrounds who are likely to hear them.

I feel now that the voices, whether they come from our own intuition or from outside entities, are actually speaking to us all, but that nowadays very few of us actually hear them. Perhaps we don't all have the need.

For me, the good thing about taking psychic guidance was that I was helped to see that there wasn't something wrong with me but rather, that I had an extra gift, an extra ability denied large numbers of people. I was enabled to see this extra dimension as something positive, rather than negative, and realize that it's not necessarily a sign of mental illness.

YOUR CHILD HAS AN IMAGINARY FRIEND

It is extremely common for children to have imaginary friends. They can happen in the most ordinary, non-psychic families and have often been regarded as a sign of disturbance in children. But, very often, it is the psychic experiences of small children that lead previously uninterested people into exploring the world of the paranormal—and discovering that there is 'something' there.

Peggy, who is now a psychic herself, was first introduced to the psychic world when her small daughter had an imaginary friend.

Laura was quite an ordinary, normal child, but from the age of about 18 months, she had a friend she called Pip. Pip would come and visit her when she was in her cot and she would hold long conversations with him. Because she was so friendly with Pip, she didn't seem to need any other little friends.

The problem was, Pip was very mischievous and always seemed to be knocking things over in her bedroom or putting her clothes and toys in different places, where they were hard to find.

I thought it was very peculiar and I had no explanation for what happened in her bedroom, but I put it down to either Laura knocking things over or one of us doing it. I knew somewhere inside myself that this couldn't be the explanation, but I don't think I wanted to look into it any further at the time.

Sometimes when I went into Laura's bedroom and found things on the floor, she would tell me that Pip put them there. Now, normally, one might imagine that the child is telling lies to get out of trouble, but often things would be misplaced or broken when she was securely in her cot and couldn't get out.

But I never investigated the matter any further or told any other members of the family. Gradually, when Laura went to school and made other friends, she seemed to forget all about Pip and stopped talking about him. I also forgot about him and don't suppose I would ever have given it another thought, except when Laura was about 17 and sitting in the living-room one evening, she suddenly said, 'I wonder whatever happened to Pip?'

At this, I felt a peculiar sensation coming over me, and remembered back to the time when Pip was so naughty, and when Laura would hold long and earnest conversations with him in her bedroom.

When I asked Laura who she meant by Pip, she looked at me in astonishment and said, 'I don't know. I don't know what made me say that.' I asked her then if she remembered she'd ever had an imaginary little friend called Pip and she said no. She was mystified.

But I felt inside myself that here was something I ought to investigate and I got in touch with the newspaper *Psychic News*. They referred me to a psychic, who explained that so-called imaginary friends are actually real people who children remember from a past life. As the memory of the past life fades, so the imaginary friend disappears as well—it's rare for these friends to last much beyond the age of four or five.

I think at the time I was ready to hear this explanation and instantly it made sense. It made me want to study psychic matters and now I am a practising clairvoyant myself.

ENGAGING IN DESTRUCTIVE BEHAVIOURAL PATTERNS

Why are you always attracted to the wrong kind of person? Why do you never seem to do what you want in life? There are two ways of approaching this problem—one is to see a psychotherapist and engage, possibly, in a lengthy analysis, and another is to see a psychic counsellor.

Sandra had been married three times and each was to a highly attractive, charismatic man who nevertheless was a philanderer. When her third marriage broke up, for the same reason as the other two, Sandra felt it was time to see a marriage guidance counsellor.

She was helpful, but I felt I needed a deeper explanation, as I didn't want to repeat the mistake. I already knew it was a pattern, but I wanted to know how to break out of it. I had read books like *Women Who Love Too Much* and found them helpful, but still I didn't feel I had got to the bottom of it.

For me, going to see a psychic counsellor helped me to piece the jigsaw together. The counsellor I saw was a gay man who looked perfectly ordinary—he was aged about 40 and wore jeans and a sweater—and he just looked at me for a few minutes before he described what he 'saw'.

He said he was getting the impression that somehow I needed to form relationships with dysfunctional men, not only because of low self-esteem, or because such men seemed normal to me, coming from an alcoholic background, but because somehow I needed to collude in their behaviour. But because I had now understood that I had kept re-enacting an ancient pattern, I had learned my lesson, and would not have the urge to form such destructive relationships in future.

The link with the past had now been broken, he told

me. The session lasted for about an hour and I didn't actually remember much of it, but he taped it for me, and every now and again I would play back the tape. I especially played it when I felt in danger of being drawn into the same type of relationship again.

I still feel slightly fragile, but when I hear those words 'You won't feel the need to repeat this behaviour in future', it gives me confidence in my own ability to form a healthier relationship in the future.

I felt I had got to the stage where I knew logically and rationally that I had been repeating an unhealthy pattern, but I hadn't got the emotional strength not to do it again. Seeing a psychic helped me to harness that strength within myself.

YOU FEEL AT A CROSSROADS

Here again, an ordinary non-psychic psychotherapist may be able to help you, but for vaguer life problems like this, an experienced psychic may be able to help you sort things out and clarify your present situation so that you can see where you might want to go—and how to go about it.

Sometimes, a psychic will ask you questions. But more often, they will look at you and tell you what they see.

Patsy, a health visitor, went to see a psychic for help with general life direction. She was feeling discontented, without knowing exactly why.

The psychic looked at me for a few minutes, and then said, 'I'm seeing a lot of people standing behind you. They are criticizing the way you do things and they're not allowing you to have enough space in your life.'

She said that I had too many people around me who

were crowding in on me and not allowing me enough emotional space. I needed more space, more privacy, she said. I allowed people to impinge on me and then resented it, but didn't know how to stop myself being a doormat.

The psychic said that actually I was a very strong woman and a bit of a perfectionist. She didn't ask me what I did for a living and had no idea that I was a health visitor. Of course, in my job I do have to see a lot of people and some of these are very demanding.

At first, I found the session very vague, as I wasn't quite sure whether the psychic was seeing members of my family or people at work. The psychic then said that it is important for all of us to keep our own space, to value our privacy and to realize that in some jobs there was a danger of burn-out, that we needed to know how to pace ourselves.

I went to see the psychic because I had been feeling dissatisfied with my job for quite a long time and was wondering whether to make a career change. I wasn't given exact guidance on this, but the fact that the psychic saw lots of people around me, taking up my time and not allowing me enough space, made me realize that I had never given enough time just to myself or ever asked myself what I really wanted.

I became a health visitor because I wanted to help people, but had never really given enough consideration to my own needs. Seeing the psychic made me ask myself some important questions and in the end I decided that I no longer wanted to be a health visitor, but do something that was purely for me.

Eventually I resigned from my job and took a course in interior design, something which had always interested me. I now work as a professional, self-employed interior designer and love the work. It fulfils my creative urge, which had been suppressed before, and I'm still meeting lots of people, as I did with health visiting.

I might have done this of course without seeing a psychic, as I had started to feel I needed a complete change from what I was doing. But that image, of the psychic seeing lots of people behind me all trying to draw strength from me and sapping my own, stayed with me. It was several years ago now that I saw the psychic, but that picture is still so powerful in my mind.

Ivan could not seem to make a success of his life, whatever he did. He had tried a series of jobs, but none of them seemed to be really 'him'. When he was made redundant, he had no idea what he wanted to do next. He had been seeing an alternative medical practitioner for chronic back problems and she suggested that he might like to see a psychic she could recommend who lived nearby. Ivan said:

One visit completely changed my life. The difference between visiting a psychic, I found, and going to see a doctor, for instance, is that psychics don't tell you what to do or give you advice. They just relate, or at least mine did, what they are receiving 'in guidance' and it's a case of if the shoe fits, wear it.

I was extremely nervous of going, because I had been brought up in a strict Catholic family and although there is a lot of mysticism and psychism in the Catholic church, we had always been told never to dabble in it ourselves, as it was the work of the devil. But the church wasn't helping me to get to the bottom of my problems, so I needed another approach.

The psychic I consulted lived in an ordinary suburban house and I was very surprised that her consulting-room was just an ordinary living-room, with plants, books, armchairs, TV and video—just like anybody else's. She was a middle-aged woman with permed hair, looking just like a receptionist at the doctor's.

I sat down opposite her and she asked me a few questions about myself. She then proceeded to tell me what the 'spirits' were conveying to her. Whether she was really in contact with spirits or tapping into my own subconscious, I don't really know, but in the end, it didn't really matter.

First of all, she—or the spirits—told me that if I was serious about wanting to get my life in order, I needed to look at my diet. At the time I was eating only junk foods. She said that I couldn't hope to look at myself in other ways unless I was prepared to eat more healthily, as unhealthy foods were addictive and prevented the mind from being clear. We are now used to this kind of advice, but at the time it was new and it sounded startling.

The next thing she said was that I had to try and give up drink. At the time, almost the only fluids I drank were alcoholic ones. I felt I needed a few drinks every day, just to function. I've never touched a drop since.

The third thing she told me was that I had to believe in karma and reincarnation as absolute facts, and that I should act as if I believed in them even if I didn't. She said that such a belief would help me to have a wider perspective, enable me to take a longer view and realize that I had to take responsibility for myself.

Once I realized all this, she said, the way ahead would become clear. Changing my behaviour and outlook was a long, hard struggle and there were many setbacks. But instead of being discouraged, I looked at the victories instead. And gradually, as I began to separate myself from unhealthy and addictive behaviour, I could see more clearly what I wanted out of life.

I had been married, but never had children, and thought that one day I would meet the right woman and we would start a family together. Through psychic guidance, I came to realize that this wasn't actually what I wanted for myself and that I didn't really want to take responsibility for children.

Eventually, I joined up with a businessman who wanted to set up stress management courses for executives. He had the business expertise, and I knew about relaxation and meditation from my contact with alternative and complementary medicine. I learned that it is never to late to change your life around and success can always come—it's a matter of attitude.

For me, psychic guidance came at the right time. I don't see psychics regularly now and in fact have little contact with that world, as our business is now so busy. But with psychic help, I was able to look at myself and clean up my act. I don't know whether I would have been able to do it completely on my own.

So far, all the stories we have heard have been successes. But don't imagine that all psychic guidance is equally good or that it can automatically help you to turn your life around. Some people professing psychic powers may genuinely want to help you, but may not have much of value to offer.

The following story illustrates what can happen when visiting a psychic who just wants to please.

Anita was rather intrigued by a psychic she met at a party. He was a middle-aged man who had held a high-ranking lecturing job until he became very ill with cancer. He had been helped by a spiritual healer and then decided to become a psychic himself.

Anita said:

I found him extremely charismatic and powerful. He was in a way slightly frightening, but intriguing at the same time. I wasn't having any particular problems at the time but, like everybody else, I felt that my life could be better, more successful.

I fixed up an appointment with him and after asking a few questions about my date of birth, star sign and everything, he started pitching in. He told me that I was going to be enormously successful, that before long I would have my own chat show on television and that everything was going to come right.

It all sounded wonderful, until I compared notes with a few other people who'd been to see him as well, and I discovered that he told everybody the same thing. Well, many years have passed and none of us have landed our own TV chat show or been conspicuously successful in the way he suggested.

I do feel he had definite psychic powers, but that what he was doing was tapping into our dreams and hopes and making us think that he could help them to come true. I don't feel that he actually was any real help, although he probably didn't do any harm, either.

Finally, here are a few dos and don'ts if you are considering seeing a psychic counsellor:

DO consider going if:
　　you genuinely feel that the psychic world is a reality;

　　you want help and guidance with difficult decisions;

　　you are ready to make changes in your life;

　　you feel able to assess and process the psychic's advice, without being unduly influenced by it;

　　you realize that you may be tapping into something extremely powerful.

DON'T consider going if:
　　you think it's all a bit of a laugh;

　　you feel psychics, mediums and clairvoyants are just barmy old ladies or weird old men;

　　you don't feel ready to take responsibility for yourself;

　　you have no good reason for visiting a psychic;

　　you just want to expose it all as so much trickery and fraud. (If you feel like this, just leave the whole thing alone, as it won't achieve anything at all.)

For those who remain intrigued, the next chapter will give more detailed questions and answers on seeing a psychic, what you can expect from a session and how to tell whether the psychic is good, bad or mediocre.

We will also take a look at an aspect of the psychic world which terrifies many people—the occult, black magic and witchcraft.

FIVE

GOING TO A COUNSELLOR

Taking any step into the unknown, especially something as 'unknown' for most people as psychic counselling, can be a very scary experience indeed. When you think that most of us find visiting the doctor, the bank manager or the dentist—ordinary, everyday people—nerve-racking enough, imagine how much more frightening it can be to consult somebody who purports to call on unseen powers, or see auras, spirits and beings which aren't, in any usually accepted sense, actually *there*.

The purpose of this chapter is to allay your fears about going to see somebody who may, at the very least, offer an extremely unusual experience. The great success of the British Festival of Mind, Body and Spirit and the various psychic fairs and conventions which are increasingly held in many parts of the world have helped to familiarize people with this area, but much remains hidden and unknown. I believe it is time for psychic advisors to take their place alongside other therapists, helpers and analysts, and for us to realize that the best of them can provide an extremely valuable service. As with anything else in life, knowledge casts out fear.

So, here are answers to the most commonly asked questions and the most frequently voiced fears about visiting a psychic.

How do I find a reputable psychic in the first place?
There is no foolproof route, but if you contact a reputable or well-established national association such as the College of

Psychic Studies or the Spiritual Association of Great Britain (SAGB), they will be able to make an appointment for you to visit somebody who has been through their vetting. This doesn't guarantee that they will be able to address your problems satisfactorily, of course, but it does mean that they are willing to work under the aegis of an umbrella organization which has stood the test of time and which has never been implicated in any questionable practices.

In Britain, the weekly newspaper *Psychic News* also has a list of clairvoyants, psychics and mediums, and may be able to help you directly if you tell them what you are looking for.

Going by personal recommendation is also a good idea, although what suits one person may not resonate with another. If you are new to psychic counselling, I would not recommend replying to an advertisement 'cold'. The psychic may be perfectly reputable, but you have no idea before you go. As you get more used to the idea, you will be better able to judge advertisements and get an idea of the person behind them.

If you ask around, you will probably find it doesn't take long before you come into contact with somebody who has consulted a psychic, and you can take it from there.

The thing is, don't be afraid to ask. You will probably be surprised at the number of people in your circle who have been to see a psychic or know somebody who has.

What qualifications should I expect a psychic to have?

There are no recognized or accredited qualifications for psychic counselling and it is difficult to see how these could be brought into being. However, the SAGB insists on 'objective evidence' of being in touch with the spirit world before it will admit a medium to its books and the College of Psychic Studies holds regular psychic development courses.

You are perfectly entitled, before fixing up a session, to ask what courses or qualifications any psychic has and also to ask to be put in touch with a satisfied client. All serious psychics should keep monitoring their own work and be in regular contact with other clairvoyants, in much the same way as psychoanalysts are always in analysis or under supervision themselves.

The great majority of psychics, although by no means all, are not educated in the formal sense, and they may have no actual academic qualifications at all. This doesn't necessarily mean they are no good, of course, as academic qualifications have no relation whatever to the psychic gift—that is something you can't learn by going on a course. You can expect them, on the whole, to be 'feeling' people rather than 'thinking' people. As they are tapping into the intuitive aspects both of themselves and of you the client, expect that the session will focus mainly on your feelings and emotions, rather than what you happen to be thinking.

Some psychics have taken formal training as counsellors or psychotherapists before discovering a psychic gift in themselves and others have trained as ordinary psychotherapists after discovering such a gift. The trend nowadays is for those with psychic gifts to take some kind of standard counselling training, so that they can gain credibility, and be on a register of qualified therapists. So you would probably find that the older the psychic, the less likely they are to have taken any formal qualification, but the younger ones frequently have degrees in psychology and diplomas in counselling.

Like any other talent, psychic ability can be honed and increased, but it can't be put there. So, the initial talent or ability is the thing that counts, but taking counselling or psychology courses shows a serious commitment and wish to help, which may instil more confidence in the novice counsellee.

What is the difference between a clairvoyant, a psychic, a medium, a sensitive and a channel?

There is not necessarily any difference at all, and mainly what psychics call themselves is a matter of personal choice.

On the whole, though, a clairvoyant is somebody who sees things (or claims to) which are hidden from most of us, while a medium or channel actually gets in touch with a spirit guide or guides and acts as a conduit through which the guides speak. (They can't speak directly, of course, as they have no bodies and no sense organs.) Channel is the American word, and medium the British word for the same thing. A sensitive is the name given in some circles to those who use ESP to gain information.

Can we take seriously these ancient Indian, Egyptian or Chinese guides that so many psychics seem to have?

Well, the psychics take them seriously enough, and very often you find when the entity is 'coming through' that everything changes and the medium seems to take on another personality. It's all a matter of assessing whether what the 'entity' is saying makes any sense or not. Mostly, people find that even if they have a job to believe in the entity, the words of wisdom and advice cannot be denied.

What happens during a typical session?

The first thing that will happen—or should—is that the counsellor will put you at your ease. Forget any fancy-dress or Madame Za Za approach—most psychics these days are very ordinary people, and will be dressed in chain-store clothes or casual jeans and trousers. I've never met one who looks like Gypsy Rose Lee—most of them take themselves far too seriously to want to dress up or seem peculiar in any way. Also, these days, they are concerned to preserve credibility. Most adhere to Bernard Shaw's dictum that if you want to say something outrageous, make sure you are conventionally dressed to say it.

Then, the session will vary depending on how the psychic works. They may ask you some questions or may ask you to sit there while they tune in and then they will do most of the talking.

Some psychics these days rely a lot on visualization and symbols to gain insights into your fears, hopes and difficulties. Veronica Stephenson has devised the 'garden game' where she asks clients who are already in a relaxed state to describe the garden of their choice. Some will have a very neat and tidy patch, while others prefer something wild and nearer to nature. The colours, choice of flowers, size of garden, safety of the area and its privacy and atmosphere will all be important in interpreting a client's state of mind and attitudes. Veronica feels that the garden game is a non-intrusive way in, as most people enjoy describing their dream garden, and find it completely non-threatening.

Other psychics may surround you with crystals, lay out a pack of cards or use astrology to help them tune into your particular wavelength. This does not always happen at once. As with traditional psychoanalysis, there may be a great deal of resistance at first and not much might be coming through.

If you feel extremely fearful and nervous, and are putting up barriers, you might come out of a session disappointed. You should not, though, feel nervous or threatened at the end of it, but as if you have achieved something, shed a burden.

You may feel slightly peculiar and disorientated on coming out of a session, but you should have a feeling of lightness and freedom as well.

I'm terrified that a psychic I contact may go into a trance. What happens here?

Actually, very little. Psychic advisors going into a trance will just go very quiet, relax and wait for the channels to be opened up. They will continue sitting in a chair, but may shut their eyes. They will be concentrating hard on what is coming through, and may even forget you are there for a time. But 'going into a trance' is far more unspectacular than most people imagine.

I'm also terrified that the psychic may put me in a trance or under hypnosis.

Most hypnotists say that it's actually impossible to hypnotize somebody against their will, although if you keep resisting you cannot expect much good to come from the session anyway. You will have to feel relaxed for the psychic to get onto your wavelength, and this may involve asking you to lie down on a couch while the psychic helps you to relax and feel at ease.

As time goes on, you will probably be aware of an altered state of consciousness, although at no time will you be 'under'. The powers of psychics to hypnotize people against their will and then make all kinds of wicked suggestions to them has been greatly exaggerated. Few people have this kind of power—unless the subject actually wants to surrender themselves in this way.

What should the psychic's consulting-room look like?

These vary enormously, from a bare room with a table and couple of chairs to a chintzy living-room. Mostly, psychics' consulting-rooms don't look too much like the average doctor's or dentist's surgery, but are more comfortable and intimate. Sometimes psychics rent rooms at alternative health centres or spiritualist organizations, and of course these are more formal and less personalized than a consulting-room in the counsellor's own home.

At the very least, the consulting-room should be clean and tidy and welcoming. It should have a calm and peaceful atmosphere, one that immediately makes you feel more relaxed. You should have a sense of ease as soon as you walk into the room.

There should be no distractions, and you should not expect the phone to ring or to be disturbed during a session, as the whole point is that the psychic is concentrating on you, and any disturbance may adversely affect this concentration.

The best psychics will be able to create an atmosphere which makes you feel as if you have come home and instantly dispels any nervousness.

How long do typical sessions last?

Usually an hour, but because of the nature of the work, because it may take time to 'make contact', it is not uncommon for them to run over. Allow an hour and a half for each session.

If at all possible, try to book sessions when you do not have to go straight back to work or into frantic preparations for a family meal. Usually, it takes a bit of time to come 'out' mentally and emotionally from a session, and it's best if you can go for a walk, go to a cafe for a cup of tea or coffee, or otherwise take time to collect your thoughts before resuming your ordinary everyday life.

One golden rule: all sessions should be taped. The reason for this is that you tend to forget what is being said and it may take time for what the psychic has said to become apparent. If the psychic has no facilities for tape recording, ask if you can take your own recorder in. This is most important, as sometimes it takes years before the truth dawns.

All psychics say that in the spirit dimension there is no time as we know it, and 'soon' can mean tomorrow, or 25 years or more. What seems 'soon' to a discarnate entity may mean a lifetime to you or I. It's a bit like the famous hymn: 'A thousand ages in thy sight, are like an evening gone'.

Psychotherapists and analysts also say that clients often don't appreciate what is being said during a session until some time afterwards, when all becomes clear. You may find that during psychic guidance, much is being said that doesn't seem to mean a great deal at the time. But if you keep the tape, you may find that the truth is gradually revealed. You may not, of course, but it's always worth keeping the tape and playing it back from time to time.

How many sessions should I have?

In many cases, one will be enough. Beware of any psychic who asks you to book up a course of sessions in advance. It is best to book up just the one and then see how you go. Some people find that all their problems are clarified during the one session, whereas others may see their psychic on a regular basis, just as they might visit the hairdresser or manicurist.

How much should I expect to pay?

At the time of writing, fees vary from around £15 an hour to £60 or £70, depending on the popularity of the psychic, the geographical situation and whether the session is held in rented rooms or in the clairvoyant's own home. It can be quite expensive—but is far cheaper than seeing a private doctor, for instance.

People often ask why psychics are not rich and the answer is that accumulating money is not where they put their energies.

At the same time, most are not poor. They are usually making an ordinary sort of living and most are very busy indeed, such is the demand these days.

How do I know whether a particular psychic is genuine?

You don't. My own personal belief, though, is that the age of fraudulent mediums, when people performed ingenious tricks while professing to see spirits, spew out ectoplasm or levitate, is over. All that sort of thing happened during the Victorian and Edwardian days when the psychic world, and investigations into apparent paranormal happenings, were new.

There can be no guarantee, however, that your psychic has amazing powers, or will shed wondrous light on a previously insoluble problem. Psychic and clairvoyant powers vary tremendously, not just from psychic to psychic, but from day to day and possibly hour to hour. As clairvoyance is a gift, to some extent it comes and goes, and cannot be guaranteed to be always the same, always on tap.

As with any profession, there are a few amazing people at the top, a large number of mediocre ones in the middle and a few at the bottom who may be no good at all. But if your practitioner has been giving readings and advice for many years, you can reasonably assume that she will have a fairly good record of success. Nobody who was useless would stay in business.

You should not expect, though, that what is being said will constitute specific advice. No psychic should ever tell you what to do, but should act as a kind of magnifying mirror to enable you to be clear about what you want. The most valuable aspect of a psychic consultation is that you are given confidence to go with your gut reaction, your intuition, even when logic and reason seem to be pointing you in the other direction.

How do I know whether a psychic is actually contacting my dead relatives or not?

You don't. There can be no absolute proof that a discarnate entity is being contacted. It may be that the psychic you visit is actually tapping into your knowledge of the person in some intuitive way. Even if they are, if nobody is actually being contacted, they may still offer startling insights and words of wisdom.

My advice is not to worry too much about whether a particular medium is really contacting some external entity, but to concentrate on whether what is being said is helpful and reassuring. If it is just banal and mundane, then there may not be any point in pursuing the matter, at least with that parti-cular psychic.

How do I know whether I am getting good advice?

There is a simple rule here: all advice and guidance which is given should be helpful and not harmful. Although no psychic should paint an impossibly rosy picture of your future, as if everything were going to be trouble-free and wonderful, there should be no negative aspects.

Otherwise, much depends on the psychic's interpretation. They will be picking up signals, either supposedly from the 'other side' or from you, and will then have to try and interpret them accurately. For instance, they might see a tall, dark figure behind you. This could be some aspect of yourself, somebody who will be helpful to you in the future or somebody who is troubling you in the present.

They will partly have to rely on their intuition to make sense of the signals they are getting from you, and partly from the information you are relaying in the way you answer the questions and your body language.

What if I'm being told patent nonsense?

Just wind up the session and put it down to experience. The problem is that anybody at all can set up as a psychic counsellor, without having any training or genuine gifts at all. If what is being said simply doesn't apply to you, or makes you feel uncomfortable or uneasy, you can feel perfectly free to say that you don't think you are getting anywhere and leave before the end of the session.

But—so often what appears to be patent nonsense makes sense months or years later. So don't be in too much of a hurry to be judgemental, but give it time. I've had psychic sessions that seemed to be revealing at the time but eventually yielded nothing and others which appeared not to apply to me at all, but where events turned out as indicated.

One of the reasons why it's often hard at first to assess whether what is being said is relevant or not is that many of us have been brought up to believe that all so-called psychic things are rubbish, so we are looking for holes and flaws.

Compare this approach to our faith in the medical establishment—we will often go along with all the tests and screens that a doctor suggests, when they are proceeding by total guesswork.

One rule of thumb here is to assess whether what is being said makes you *feel* anything. In the psychic world, feelings are the ultimate reality, and if you get a knot in your stomach or some other indication that what is being said directly applies to you, then you can take heed. If you get used to seeing psychics, you will gradually become used to trusting and going with your feelings. In fact, my belief is that this is really what psychic guidance is all about—enabling you to trust your deepest feelings and instincts, rather than trying to overrule them.

Many psychics believe that, in some part of our being, we all know what we should do, what is best for us, but that we often override this intuitive information because it's not what we want to hear or think we ought to hear. As we learn to go with our feelings, we will find life goes more the way we want it.

For instance, when I fell deeply and instantly in love with a man I had not even met, I got a flash, a warning that this would never work out. But I could not go with that feeling, and caused myself untold anguish as a result. I needed psychic counselling to get over it, many years later.

As we become more tuned into the deepest aspects of ourselves, we get 'touchings' or gut feelings which we learn to obey, because they are right for us. We learn to have less hesitation about taking the right course of action and to be confident about taking risks.

A good psychic will enable you to gain confidence to trust yourself, and know instinctively what is right for you.

With so much variety in the psychic world, how do I choose the best type of counsellor for me?

The only thing you can do here is to go with your instincts. If you like playing cards, you may be intrigued by the idea of cartomancy. If you love and are fascinated by crystals, a crystal healer may be right for you. If you prefer a more academic approach, you may like to go to somebody with an academic background. If you are intrigued by the prospect of contacting the other side, choose a medium who uses this method.

One good way of assessing your reaction to psychic matters is to wander round a festival or fair and see what attracts you. Some people like colour, incense and a feeling of sensuality while others prefer a more austere approach.

I'm interested in attending a spiritualist church. What happens?

In general, spiritualist churches follow a similar pattern to that of other church services in that they have readings, hymns and prayers. The difference is that instead of a sermon, there will be some demonstration of clairvoyance. Very often, the congregation is made up of people who wish to contact those who have passed over to the other side and the clairvoyant will attempt to contact them.

Many people go to spiritualist churches, at least for a few times, for fun, and leave it there. (Details of your local church should be listed in the telephone directory.) On the whole, in my experience, the standard of clairvoyance at the average small-town spiritualist church is not high, but you can be pleasantly surprised. You will find that the rest of the congregation is made up of extremely ordinary looking people—and you may be surprised at how commonplace it all seems.

What sort of practices are unacceptable?

It should go without saying that any suggestion of any sexual contact between you and the psychic is absolutely out. Just recently, disturbing information has come to light showing that many male therapists and analysts have had sexual relations with their female clients. There is as yet little data on whether the same may happen the other way round, although as most psychoanalysts are male, it would necessarily be rarer.

Any kind of intimate contact at all, even hugging and kissing, is unacceptable. Some counsellors ask you to sit in a chair opposite them, while others prefer you to lie down on a bed or couch. There is nothing wrong with this, although on no account should you agree to take your clothes off or engage in any sexual practices whatever. The whole point of psychic sessions is that they should put you at your ease, not make you feel uncomfortable.

You should not take any notice of a psychic who advises you to have lots of affairs, suggests ways to try and increase your virility or sexual appeal, or promises you will have power over others. The only power one should gain by seeing a psychic is power over oneself, and a sense of control over one's own life. Anything else is unacceptable and nobody who purports to help you increase your sphere of influence or infiltrate secret circles is to be trusted.

All practising therapists know that it is common for clients and patients to fall in love with them and imagine that they are some kind of oracle or guru and can do no wrong. Then, later, disillusionment sets in. A good psychic counsellor should, as with any other type of counsellor, discourage any personal relationship or contact other than the purely professional.

What is the danger of inadvertently getting into the occult, or black magic?

Very slight. Although dabbling in the occult and black magic undoubtedly goes on, it is probably more confined to films and books than real life. The main point of black magic practices seems to be sexual, to conjure up sexual potency, and as we have said before, there should be no sexual connotation of any kind with psychic counselling.

Over the years I have seen and interviewed very many psychic counsellors and advisors and have never once come across one who uses any form of black magic, however mild. Present day Aleister Crowleys probably do exist, but they are not people the general public are likely to contact.

Why are most mediums women or gay men?

This is because psychic powers are intimately allied to the
feminine, to the receptive and intuitive rather than reasoning,
logical and aggressive aspects. The very best mediums,
however, make use of both. It can be as dangerous to be all
'feeling' as it can to be all apparent reason and logic. We need
both love and law, emotions and discrimination.

There is also the aspect that women and gay men are, on the
whole, more open generally about psychic matters, alternative
and complementary medicine and all new ideas in these areas.

Most of the ghost-hunters are, or have been, men, but these
are usually men looking for incontrovertible evidence of the
existence of ghosts, rather than people who have any
psychic gifts.

Why are most mediums middle-aged, at least?

Although the psychic faculty is there right from early years,
certainly pre-school, it tends to disappear with age and by the
age of seven it has often died down completely. This is, say
psychics, because our educational system is so left-brain
oriented and because so little importance is given to psychic
aspects of life in our society today.

Very often, children who have exhibited psychic powers
when very young learn to keep quiet about them because
they are laughed at or not believed. Then 'real life' takes over
and they go to school, university, get jobs, get married, have
families and live ordinary domestic lives. It is often not until
middle age, not until all those aspects are once more out of the
way, that the psychic faculty becomes apparent again. There is
also a school of thought which says that psychic powers are in
abeyance during an active sex life and that it is only when
sexuality becomes less important that they can emerge again.

There is another school of thought, however, which
maintains that psychic awareness can be heightened during
sexual activity. However, for most women, it seems that
psychic faculties only emerge again when intense sexuality has

died down. For possibly the same reason, most practising male psychics tend to be older men, those who are content to let the sexual aspect of themselves take second place.

Another reason why most psychics tend to be older people is that with increasing age comes increasing confidence, and they don't care so much about what other people might think. So they gain more courage to acknowledge and use their psychic gift.

Are spiritual healers psychic?

Yes—the psychic ability and the healing ability are part of the same gift. The essence of the psychic gift is that it makes things whole, harmonious. Most psychics feel that there is some kind of energy coming through them when they practise their art and that this energy enables them to heal.

Healing is usually practised at a mental level. It is becoming an increasingly important use of psychic abilities. Ever more doctors and health centres are employing spiritual healers and they have now gained a respectability which they certainly did not have in the early part of the century.

Are newspaper astrologers genuinely psychic and can we take any notice of them?

Well, they all take their work extremely seriously, and for almost all, the newspaper work is only a small aspect of their involvement with psychic matters.

On the whole, the downmarket newspaper astrologers concentrate on the good things of life, while those in the more 'respectable' newspapers and magazine issue warnings and cautions, telling us not to expect that everything will be wonderful or that love, luck and money are coming our way. Newspaper astrology, however, by its nature, is extremely general and cannot necessarily be expected to apply directly to you.

Can psychics predict who will win the Derby, for example?

Only if they are particularly interested in racing and have made a detailed study of it. Most psychics don't concern themselves with such things, as they feel it is a misuse of their powers.

What about predictions? Can they be believed?

Again, most reputable psychics don't concern themselves with specific predictions. Sometimes they get vivid dreams or premonitions about what will happen, but usually they are not believed anyway!

Sometimes the police use psychics to help them in their work to trace missing persons, but, it has to be said, not with a great deal of success.

In order to make an accurate prediction, there has to be some kind of contact with the person or event, a message sent and received by some means.

One problem also with making predictions is that nobody knows what time-scale we are talking about. A predicted event could happen tomorrow or in 10 years. Some psychics may be very specific—foretelling, for example, that you will have two children, both boys, and that you will marry a foreigner who will die after you have been together 30 years. But predictions of this nature are not the most useful reason for visiting a psychic. Also, they take away an element of free will—if I know exactly how my life is going to be mapped out, I may then try to make it happen.

Psychics can be useful in giving general trends and probabilities, by tuning into your character and aspirations. But they should not give you chapter and verse as to what will happen. They don't know, anyway, any more than you do.

What about curses? Can they come true?

Literature and folklore are full of stories about people who put curses on others—the wicked fairy is an obvious example—and some people would say that curses work to this day. The poet Kathleen Raine put a curse on the man she loved, *Ring of Bright Water* author Gavin Maxwell, and his life never went right again. Seven years later, he was dead. As she uttered the curse, Raine had the strong feeling that she had ushered in an inexorable course of events and that the curse could not be reversed.

Undoubtedly, there are strong negative energies around and we may need all the positive thinking we can muster to circumvent them. But whatever the truth, any so-called psychic who issues curses should be avoided. Reputable psychics are not in the business of muttering curses. Their job is to harmonize, make clear and connect, rather than dissipate, destroy or harm.

SIX

PSYCHIC COUNSELLING IN RELATIONSHIPS

The famous astrologer and psychic Patric Walker has said that people worry mainly about three things: jobs, money and relationships. Of those, I would say that the major worry is about relationships—and always has been. All great literature, painting, music, philosophy and religion is, ultimately, about relationships: our relationship with ourselves, with God, with our parents, our children, our lovers, husbands and wives, our neighbours and workmates, with the world around us, with the universe, with animals and pets, with our homes and possessions, with our bodies, our minds, our emotions, our attitudes.

We all want to have good relationships with everybody. We want to feel happy and at peace with ourselves. Yet, somehow, few of us seem able to manage it. Why is this—and how can psychic counsellors help?

One of the main jobs of a good psychic counsellor is to enable the clients to see what part they have played, and are playing, in their important relationships, and to help them take responsibility for their own actions and for what they set in motion.

In a sense, money and jobs are also aspects of our relationships. We have to know what is our relationship to money, what is our relationship to our job or career before we can make sense of it—or understand why money or the absolute right job always seems to elude us.

Of course, it is not always necessary to see a psychic counsellor to gain clarification of these issues. Sometimes talking to a friend or seeing some other type of counsellor will do the trick. Sometimes all we need to do is to ask ourselves what we want—and the answer comes quickly. What the psychic approach can do is to help us to see the particular energies around certain key aspects of our lives, so that we can trust ourselves to make appropriate decisions.

YOUR RELATIONSHIP WITH YOURSELF

I've put this first because it is easily the most important. Unless you can have a good relationship with yourself, unless you can like and feel positive about yourself, you can hardly expect to have good relationships with other people.

Very often, the ending of an important intimate relationship may be the catalyst for a good hard look at ourselves. Everything proceeds from that.

Psychic Philippe Raynaud says: 'Things that look terrible when they happen may actually be the best thing to happen. They can be the starting-point for a new look at oneself, a new look at life. Sometimes, the old has to be destroyed before the new can be built up.'

By reflecting back to you the information you psychically convey, a clairvoyant may be able to help you to see more clearly who you really are, what you want and where you are going.

And never imagine that to go to a psychic for 'selfish' reasons is a waste of time. In our current 'New Age', people have been criticized for navel-gazing, looking inwards and focusing on themselves rather than the wider problems of society. The question often arises: 'Why are you spending (wasting) all this money on yourself when you could be giving it to Oxfam and helping the starving millions? Why are you spending all this time concentrating on yourself when we have so many homeless, so many people out of work, so many people unhappy and miserable?'

The point here is that it is actually impossible to offer any genuine help to others unless you have first got yourself in order. The phrase 'Physician, heal thyself' should apply to all of us. Before we can be of any real use to other people, before we can hope to have good relationships, we need to sort ourselves out. It's no good just having vague impulses of helping others without knowing why we do it or what we—or they—may hope to gain by it. We have to understand our own motives and be very clear about what we are setting in motion and what is likely to be the result.

And sometimes a psychic, somebody who looks at life with another kind of vision, can be just the person to help you get to know yourself, and face the future with confidence and serenity.

INTIMATE RELATIONSHIPS

We have been given to understand that the most important thing in life is to form an intimate relationship, preferably with somebody of the opposite sex, and preferably with the same person for life. Because this is currently seen as such an ideal, we make strenuous attempts to make our personal relationships work. We are advised to put 'commitment' into them. Yet the sad fact is that hardly any of them do work, at least in the long term.

One of the reasons for this is that we tend to grow up having expectations of other people and are then disappointed when they don't behave as we would like them to. Also, most of us try to conform to some kind of sentimental ideal, without ever asking ourselves whether this is right for us or whether it's what we actually want.

We are not all the same. Some of us are loners, some of us are 'natural' pairers-up with people, some of us are naturally monogamous while others find it impossible to sustain a relationship with one person for the rest of their lives. Also, we have different sexual needs. Some of us find it enormously empowering and liberating not to have any sexual contact at all, while for others expression of sexuality constitutes an essential aspect of life.

We can have healthy relationships both with ourselves and others when we can understand who we are and what we want, and then fulfil our own destiny without hurting or shaming or using others. If we do not want to do ourselves any harm, it is unlikely we will have the motivation to harm others.

A common cry in relationships is: 'I'd be all right if only he/she would change!' One major aspect of all relationship counselling is to enable people to see that they can't change others, and that they have to concentrate on their own attitude if they want their relationships to improve. All professional counsellors understand this, but sometimes this revelation comes more dramatically from a psychic than from other types of counsellor, as they can 'see', sometimes in almost tangible form, what you are supposed to be like, and how other people are affecting you.

Some psychics say that when they are holding sessions, they see the person in front of them not as they are at the moment, but as how they could be. They visualize an ill person as somebody in perfect health, as the best of themselves, whatever others might see to the contrary. It is this ability to see perfection rather than the present imperfections that gives the very best clairvoyants the 'edge' over other types of therapist.

Sometimes, of course, a relationship will be at an end anyway, and a consultation with a psychic may help you to clarify this—and see into your future.

Pauline was devastated when her husband left her for a younger woman. It was a common enough scenario, but Pauline and Rick had built up their employment agency business together, and she could hardly believe it when Rick rang her up one day and told her he'd fallen in love with

Amanda, the young assistant Pauline had hired and had been grooming for an eventual executive job within the company.

I was 46, and like so many women, had been brought up to believe that my most outstanding achievement would be to land a husband. Rick was dashing, handsome and confident when I met him, and we'd worked together for nearly 20 years to build up our business into the success it had become.

I felt that at my age I would never meet anybody else, but couldn't see how I was ever going to manage on my own. I thought about computer dating and then a friend asked me if I'd ever considered trying to find a partner through astrological matchmaking. Apparently, this was a way of finding your ideal partner through the stars.

I felt I had nothing to lose, so I booked up a session with an astrological counsellor. What emerged was quite extraordinary. The counsellor drew up my chart and started asking me questions. She said that she saw somebody who was actually meant to be on her own, somebody for whom marriage or similar long-term partnership was not indicated.

I felt very cross and disappointed at this, as I had hoped to set something in motion which would help me find my ideal partner. Other things which emerged from the astrological reading were that my marriage had actually been over for many years, but because I clung on to the status of being a wife and the illusion of a happy marriage, I had not ever looked at what I really wanted.

I began to realize that there was some truth in what was coming out and that I never had questioned the concept of getting married and having children. But when I thought about it a bit more, I somehow knew that I was not a 'natural' wife. I had told myself I was in love with Rick, and I had tried all the conventional things to make the marriage last, such as working together, making sure he had a nice home, meals on the table and trying to be sexy in bed.

It came home to me with a startling clarity some time later that this wasn't at all what I had wanted. And although I hadn't chosen to become single or wanted him to go off with another woman, I came to understand that, far from being a terrible tragedy, it actually enabled me for the first time in my life to see what I wanted.

Several years have gone by now. Rick and I got divorced, we disbanded the joint business and I set up on my own. After a few years of struggle and uncertainty, the business is now going well, and I am happy to be in charge. I also realized that in fact I and not Rick was the business head.

The years of being on my own have enabled me to expand my consciousness, to study all kinds of areas which had been closed before, because I was trying to play a conventional role. I'm not knocking marriage guidance or any other form of marital counselling, but I doubt whether it would have helped me see myself so clearly as the astrological reading.

The whole point of having good relationships is that you are able to connect, to have empathy with the other person, to see them as both separate from yourself and as part of the same jigsaw. Jigsaws make pictures with interlocking pieces and yet all are separate. They may merge into one, but you can always see the demarcation lines. One jigsaw piece is not exactly the same as another, and you can take it out and let it stand on its own at any time. Yet it won't make a pretty picture by itself. As humans, and as part of nature, part of the universe, we all interlock, and yet we have our separate identities.

The idea of connectedness has been widely misinterpreted. It does not mean being glued together, having no idea where you might end and another person begin, and it does not mean dependence and attachment, often confused with genuine love. It means, rather, being able to see yourself as a separate person in order to connect properly. It means not taking on other people's negative thinking and habits, or being emotionally affected by what they do. It means realizing that they act as they do because of what they are—and not because of you.

For example, you might have a lover who is consistently late for appointments. It's easy to start thinking, 'If she really loved me, really cared, she'd be on time rather than keep me waiting.' This attitude means that you start to blame her for being late and begin to resent the time you are kept waiting. Then when she eventually arrives you are in a rage and the evening gets off to a bad start.

What is actually happening, by contrast, is that she's late because she's late—and it has nothing to do with you. She'd be just as late for any other lover, and if you decide to get annoyed, that is up to you. Being late is part of her problem—if it is seen as a problem—not something she does to spite and confuse you. Because punctuality causes so very much trouble in many relationships, we'll look at the dynamics involved.

People who are always late are those who try to pack too many activities into too short a time, not giving themselves long enough to get ready and get to the place or meeting on time. It is all to do with self-respect, pacing themselves, understanding how long jobs may take or how long a journey might take. It's nothing to do with anyone waiting for them—it's how they are and you have no power to change them. Persistent lateness is a complicated matter which has nothing to do with 'having no sense of time'. If the late person really had no sense of time, they'd be as often early as late.

A psychic counsellor explained the psychology behind chaotic timekeeping:

When people are always late, it may seem as if they are saying, 'I'm more important than you, so I'll keep you waiting.' In fact, those who are consistently late are usually highly nervous people who are worried about turning up at all. They are late because they have little self-confidence. And if they try to pack too much in, not giving themselves enough time to get ready, this means they don't value themselves enough to take the proper amount of time. They don't value themselves properly, therefore they can't see what they might be doing to the other person by keeping them waiting. In a sense, they are testing the other person as well, and saying, 'If you really loved me, you wouldn't mind waiting.'

The lateness scenario is symbolic of the pain we can put ourselves and others in—when actually there is no need for it.

Michaela was always so late for appointments that it had cost her several love affairs. Eventually, when she lost somebody who she imagined would wait for her for ever, she sought counselling for her problem. She said:

> I didn't just see the counsellor for lateness, but to try and discover why my relationships never seemed to last or work out properly. All my boyfriends left me in despair— and I couldn't see why.
>
> One of the things that emerged was my terrible lateness problem. The counsellor asked me why I always felt I had to be late, and eventually I came to the realization that I never saw myself as important enough to give myself enough time to get ready or to get to a place on time. I would mess about doing other things, and then, when the time came to be there, would think about getting ready. Now, I get myself ready first and then see what time I have left over for other things.
>
> Since I conquered my lateness tendency, I find my relationships have gone better than ever before. I'm not testing people, not testing myself, and can forget about all that manipulative behaviour. Because I've now got a better view of myself, I have more respect for others, and this means I need no longer play games.

Psychic counsellors may also be able to help us to see that

we always set in motion the kind of relationships that in some way we need to have. They may not be comfortable, fulfilling or exciting—but they spring from our own need, our own personalities, our own attitudes. They don't just happen by chance. We have to realize that if we fall in love with dysfunctional people, those who treat us badly, it's because in some deep way we have *chosen* to fall in love with them, for our own reasons. One of the most important lessons that can be learned through psychic counselling is that we must take responsibility for all our relationships and never blame the other person. They are what they are and if we don't like it then we must adjust our attitudes or decide to end the relationship.

Mostly, relationships continue because both parties are getting something out of them, some kind of satisfaction, even when it may not look like that to others.

Sadie had a very unhappy marriage. She was married to a man whose alcoholism eventually made him mentally ill. Always unstable and unpredictable, he had turned into a kind of monster, locking her out of the house, hitting her, making threats, having affairs, being sick down the stairs on Saturday nights and then abusive and moody for the rest of the week.

Nobody who knew her understood how she could put up with it, especially as she was herself a successful businesswoman, the breadwinner. She didn't need Albert's money to survive. Yet the years went by and she continued to be married to him. One by one, all her friends deserted her as they could not stand him. Her children urged her to leave him, as they hated him too. Yet she never did leave him, even though she did nothing but complain about him to whoever would listen. Sometimes, she and Albert didn't speak for weeks. They had gone into separate bedrooms years before and never went on holiday or to any social functions together. It all seemed inexplicable.

Then one day a friend with whom Sadie was on holiday suggested seeing a psychic, 'for fun'. Sadie soon started complaining about her terrible husband to the psychic, who then told her what she at the time didn't want to hear.

Sadie said:

She told me that the reason I stayed with him was because I wanted to, and that I had colluded in and encouraged his bad behaviour so that I could feel superior, feel a victim, a martyr.

At first, I couldn't take this at all. I had expected the psychic to be sympathetic and here she was telling me that I had played a part in it and that I was enjoying the role of martyr. She also told me that I had for some reason 'needed' to have such a relationship, when all my life I had seen myself as the passive victim, the wronged wife of a horrible man.

The psychic said that if my life really was that terrible, I'd have left him, yet somehow I didn't want to. She told me that we were, in some way, bound together, for karmic reasons. The relationship was giving each of us a chance to work something out. Well, at the time I resisted it completely and felt the psychic was talking nonsense.

After the session, my friend said she thought there was a lot of truth in what the psychic had said, but I wasn't convinced. Gradually, though, over the years, I came to realize that I had to take responsibility for my relation-ships and if they didn't work out or made me unhappy, it was up to me to try and discover why.

I never did find the courage to leave my husband but not long after that, he died from chronic alcohol abuse, or so the doctor said. I think that the years without him have been my happiest, but in a funny kind of way I miss him. Perhaps some part of me did need the violence, the abuse, the terrible rows—although I would have died at the time rather than admit it.

We always choose what we do, although it's often hard to come to terms with the realization that we may 'want' to form relationships with people who are no good for us and who don't make us happy.

For example, you may have fallen in love with a philanderer. It's useless to hope that the love of a good woman will make him see the error of his ways and change them. For him, philandering is the nature of the beast. You can decide not to have a relationship with such a person, or you can, as with the lateness, decide not to let it spoil the good things about your relationship. It's no use hoping that if you look sexy enough, if you are available enough, if you are around him enough, he will reform. He won't.

Many of us sabotage ourselves because, deep down, we don't imagine we are worthy of the best, that we deserve a good relationship, to be nurtured and supported.

Very few psychic counsellors believe in the 'passive victim' mentality, or that we get ourselves into a mess through no fault of our own. Although 'fault' is a word most people in the psychic world would hesitate to use, there is the understanding that if we form dysfunctional relationships, if we take up with people who abuse us or treat us badly, that in some way we have 'chosen' to do this. And until we can realize this, we will be powerless to change our behaviour. But once we realize what we have been doing, seeing a psychic can help to set in motion more helpful patterns of behaviour.

One of my first sessions ever with a psychic counsellor helped me to realize that I had enacted a pattern of self-sabotage over the years and that this had prevented me from achieving what appeared to be my full potential. I found it painful, but a very valuable insight. I also realized that, in some cases, unhelpful patterns of behaviour go back very many years.

I was lying on a couch and the counsellor was regressing me to childhood, to the age of 10 or 11. I started to remember very vividly an incident in my last year at primary school.

The headmaster of the school every year held a competition for the best pressed wild flower collection, with a small monetary prize. A few of us went in for the competition and as the weeks went by it became clear that my entry was by far the best. Not only did it have more wild flowers than anybody else's collection, but I had taken care to identify them correctly, even giving them all their Latin names. Yet, when it came time to hand the collection in, I 'lost' mine. I never handed it in and I didn't win the prize, which went to a collection that was nothing like as good as my own.

Why had I needed to do this? I couldn't imagine. Yet, when this memory was uncovered, I realized it formed a pattern: never had I thought I was good enough for the best, so I unconsciously sabotaged my own actions.

It was a pattern which meant that I never did as well as school as I could have done (should have done), never got into the university of my choice and that my first real love affair was a disaster. To some extent, I had managed to reverse the pattern with advancing years, but there was always the feeling at the back of my mind that I didn't deserve the best, that I should settle for second best. Others could take the glittering prizes, I would have the ones left behind and never *quite* make it, because of my attitude about myself.

I hope that uncovering this tendency has meant that I no longer do this, but through psychic counselling I came to understand the reason for my often not winning the prize, not going after the very best that I was capable of, but settling for something below my full potential.

As we form patterns of behaviour, so we tend to form relationships with the same type of people, often not realizing that we do this—or why we might do it. Psychic counsellors can often help us to see why and enable us to harness the tendency for our own good, instead of letting it work against us.

Sonya did not realize there was a pattern in her relationships until she sought psychic counselling. She wondered why she had never in her life been attracted to, or gone out with, a rich man, and what it was about certain types of men that intrigued

her. At the time, there were no particular problems. It had just
come home to her that there *was* such a pattern and she
wanted to try to get to the bottom of it. She felt it could not be
chance that every important man in her life was of a similar
type.

If you lined them up in an identity parade, it would seem
as if they had nothing in common. Certainly not in
physical appearance. I have been equally attracted to tall,
dark handsome men, tall, fair handsome men and short
men who weren't handsome at all. Some have been the
same age as me, some younger, some a great deal older.
And they haven't all come from the same kind of
background or had a similar education.

But with the help of psychic counselling, I began to
realize that I was always attracted to the same type—a
man with high intelligence, who was witty and amusing,
with a great sense of humour, but at the same time
somebody who was a bit of a maverick, who never fitted
into the conventional world and who also had a rather
tenuous connection with the world of work—because of
what I was like. I put out certain vibes and a particular
type of man responded. Others didn't respond at all and
neither did I warm to them, even though in practical
terms some might have been better bets than the ones I
was attracted to.

All the important men in my life, I realized, were people who had not had a consistent or clear career pattern,
in the sense of climbing up a well-established ladder. But
they were always verbally adept, able to describe their
emotions and were people who treated women as equal
human beings, rather than status symbols, adjuncts or
household slaves.

All of the men I've been wildly attracted to have been
interested in ideas, in philosophy, art, music, religion.
They've been open-minded and alive to new ideas. Also,
there's always been a bit of the boy, a bit of them that's

never grown up and retains an interest in toy soldiers, video games, adventures—whatever.

Just recently, I was powerfully attracted to a man I met at a party. When I got to know him a bit, I realized with some bemusement that he was exactly the same type as the others—witty, clever, self-deprecating, talented yet unsure of himself, and again, somebody who had never had a conventional career pattern. I wasn't even looking for a relationship or hoping to meet anybody, yet it happened. The same pattern all over again!

Seeing a psychic enabled me to realize that I was the sort of person for whom it was important to earn my own living. I had never been attracted to rich men because I didn't want them to have that kind of power over me.

I wanted an equal relationship, and the fact that so many men I liked were not rich or big earners meant that I was happy to take financial responsibility for myself and would never expect anybody else to keep me or provide for me.

I realized that we can probably not break the pattern of our relationships, but we can come to see that it is a pattern and make it work for us once we become conscious of it. I also came to understand that, very often, the reason that relationships don't work is because we are trying to pair up with the sort of person we feel we ought to, rather than the kind who genuinely resonates with us.

Like so many women, I've always had an idea at the back of my mind that I would like to feel financially secure, that in some part of my being I would like somebody to provide for me. What I now realize is that I would absolutely hate this and couldn't bear to pay the price.

Another related pattern I was enabled to see was that, although I kept saying that I wanted financial security—I run a PR agency and life is always on the edge—in fact, I didn't really want this at all. If I had wanted it, somehow I would have arranged it for myself.

But in order to keep myself working, to keep on the

ball, to keep looking for new accounts and trying to give the very best I could, I kept getting myself in situations where financial worries loomed. The psychic I saw said that if I genuinely wanted a quiet, easy life I could get a job in a library or as somebody's secretary, buy or rent a modest house and not look for anything else.

But it's never been enough and I seem to have to keep facing new challenges. I have never felt secure in my finances and have compounded this by being attracted to men without any money. But at the same time, I do sometimes make a lot of money. It's just not that consistent.

Ellen, by contrast, did marry a rich man. He was seven years older, much better educated than she was, and provided an extremely comfortable lifestyle where she was able to have a huge house, lots of foreign holidays, nannies and au pair girls and cleaners and private education for their three children. And she didn't have to lift a finger! Perfection, some might think. A dream come true.

But over the years Ellen came to feel that the relationship was ever more imbalanced as Steve earned more money and climbed up the executive ladder. Eventually, he became very rich indeed. Yet whenever she tried to even up the situation somewhat, by getting a job herself or taking courses to become qualified in a profession, there was resentment and accusations that she wasn't being a good wife, and didn't she have everything she wanted without wanting to go out to work? It wasn't as if they needed the money, anyway, he would say when she wasn't available to accompany him on a foreign trip or demurred at entertaining his business colleagues.

Ellen became interested in alternative medicine and eventually in psychic matters. She made an appointment with a psychic counsellor to see if there was any way her relationship could be improved or whether she might be able to get out of it. As she had never earned any money of her own since getting married and there was no possibility that she could earn anything like the amounts Steve brought in, there was real fear when she contemplated a life without him. But she was beginning to hate him. She said:

> I found it very painful indeed going to see a psychic, because it meant I had to look at what part I had played in the relationship and take responsibility for my own actions.
>
> I was helped to see that I had actually married Steve because of his money, or at least because of the expectation that one day he would be a big earner, which in fact he was. A lot of high-earning men believe that if they provide everything, as they see it, that their wives should be happy and they can't see why they're not.
>
> I had been blaming Steve for insensitivity, for not seeing what I wanted, but had not wanted to acknowledge that I had been colluding in the relationship or that I had chosen this type of person for my own reasons.
>
> Once I was able to accept that I had been colluding, that actually we had been dovetailing together, then I could have a different view of the marriage. I learned to stop being angry at Steve, and to look at myself and my own decisions instead. I have never in my adult life had any money worries, but instead, I realized that I didn't know exactly who I was, that I didn't have a clear sense of my own identity. Also, because I had always been financially dependent, I was emotionally dependent as well and had never really grown up. I'd never had to.

Through psychic counselling, Ellen understood that she was not ready to leave Steve, that she did not feel able to cope on her own and that the money he brought in was important to her. She persuaded Steve to go for psychic counselling as well—the marriage had got so bad that he was prepared to consider anything—and they worked through their problems together.

Psychic counsellor Philippe Raynaud said:

Once people realize that they have been colluding in a relationship, that it's pointless to blame, their eyes are opened. It is always helpful if partners can come together, although this can be difficult to arrange, as very often it's only one who is ready to look at themselves and try to see how old patterns of behaviour can be improved.

When people come to me, I'm able to see why they are the way they are, often when they can't see it themselves. I can also maybe help them to see that a situation which looks terrible may in fact be the best thing that can happen, as it acts as a catalyst for growth and change. Most of us resist change as we would rather stick to what we know, and I would say it's probably not worth seeing a psychic counsellor for help with relationships unless you are prepared to look at yourself and consider changing your behaviour or attitudes.

It would be ridiculous to suggest that we can never embark on a relationship without first having a consultation with a psychic counsellor or that such people can make everything clear and plain sailing. But sometimes, a timely word or suggestion can put something which seems strange into a perspective which helps us to cope and make sense of the situation.

Since splitting up from her husband *Tina* had lived for five years on her own and was very happy with her new life. She had never had another relationship and, because she was embarking on a medical course as a mature student, did not feel she had room or time in her life for anybody else, particularly a lover.

Then she met Martin. She fell deeply in love with him and he with her. But he had also been living on his own for several years and valued his freedom. As a writer, he liked to travel a lot and did not want any encumbrances which might keep him anchored in one particular place. Sometimes he was away for months on end and just kept a small flat going to which he would return to write his books. At 50, he had never been married and never had a long-term relationship, although he had often been in love. But rather than settle for the domestic life, he had always valued his freedom highly.

Tina said:

Neither of us wanted this relationship and yet it happened. I knew that a friend of mine, a former work colleague when we were both teachers, had trained as a psychic counsellor and I thought I would confide in her.

She said that sometimes we need to live in a comfort zone and that was what I had been doing for the past five years. But, she added, we can't live in a comfort zone forever, and sometimes we have to go out into the world and test what we have learned.

To her, it seemed clear that somewhere in the cosmos it was ordained that I should have another relationship, and that it should be both passionate and equal, a relationship such as I'd never had before. I was very clear in my own mind that, for the time being at least, I did not want to clutter up my life with somebody else permanently around, but that having this new lover gave me the chance to see how I coped with an intimate affair.

Because of what she told me, I had the courage and confidence to carry on. I just let it happen, enjoying it for today and not thinking about tomorrow. In the past, I'd either have wanted some firm commitment or felt the whole thing was a waste of time.

It was a new experience to me to learn that we could enjoy each other's company without any strings being attached, without trying to extract promises or vows, just letting it happen for the present.

For the first time in my life, I had an affair which made me feel happy and positive, rather than miserable and clinging. I learned to my surprise that I could handle a relationship, that it could be light and easy, and that we didn't have to become a 'couple' or forgo any of our former activities.

In the past, I'd have felt that if I was going out with somebody, I would have to do everything with them—go to the cinema, the theatre, dinner parties, restaurants—and that I would have to curtail my other activities, forget about my other friends.

This time, though, it didn't happen. I kept all my other activities going, my work didn't suffer—and it was just another delightful dimension. I don't want to marry Martin or to live with him, but we can come together when he's in this country and just enjoy each other's company. At one time, I would never have thought such an easy relationship with a member of the opposite sex was possible and it's been a delightful realization.

Psychic awareness can help us to see that we can fall in love at any age, that although the body visibly ages, the soul or spirit is ageless, and that when we meet somebody new, it is so that we can learn important lessons about ourselves and others. We can understand that there is a reason for everything, that things are not set in motion by caprice or mere chance. Everything is part of the jewelled movements of our lives.

Above all, I think, psychic awareness enables us to have love and compassion for ourselves and for all other human beings and creatures. It enables us to reach out to other people, to have the confidence to offer them the hand of friendship and say, or at least imply, 'You are my brother or sister.'

It enables us to wish others well and to let the monsters of envy and greed disappear from our lives. When these go, a huge burden goes with them. We learn to detach, to see things with a wider view. We can learn to say, 'This is me and that is them, and we each have a different destiny to fulfil. I am not "better" than you, and you are not "better" than me—just different.'

Obviously, psychic counselling is not needed at every stage of our life, or every time we embark on a new relationship or consider ending an old one. It would be ridiculous to suggest that you can never take any course of action without first consulting a clairvoyant. I would say the time to consider seeing a psychic or clairvoyant is when you are confused about which way to turn next and would welcome some clarification. You might like to look back at Chapter 4 to revise when it might be a good idea to consult a psychic.

Psychic counselling can often help you to see the energies around certain activities and relationships, and work out what to do for the best. But you have to be ready. Some people are not ready to take responsibility for themselves or their actions and there would be little point in them seeing a psychic. For example, you might feel that the time has come to take a cool look at your relationship, but your partner might believe everything is going perfectly and that the last thing that's needed is anything to rock the boat.

Carla had felt dissatisfied with her marriage for very many years and eventually saw a psychic counsellor for help.

He told me that the energy he saw around the relationship was that I desperately wanted to leave, but that I was afraid of hurting my husband's feelings.

I very much wanted to discuss what the counsellor had said, but I couldn't persuade him either to listen or to come with me to the counsellor. Eventually I felt I had no choice but to leave him as I felt stifled in the marriage.

He never understood it and I felt very sad that he wouldn't even come with me for counselling. It was a very hard lesson for me to learn that although I was ready, he wasn't—and that there was no way I could make him see my new point of view.

Years later, he still doesn't see what went wrong and believes that with a bit more 'give and take', as he calls it, it could have worked. But what I've seen is that although I have changed so much, he hasn't changed at all and is still not ready to look at himself in any way.

He soon remarried and embarked on another family. I can see that he is repeating the pattern of our relationship with his new wife, but he can't, and it's not up to me to point it out, or try to get him to see this.

What makes me really sad is that his new wife is going through all the problems I went through in trying to cope with him. It's as if he has learned nothing—but I have to realize that he has his own destiny to fulfil and that I have my own quite separate one.

I thought that we had a good marriage and that was how it seemed to outsiders. But inside, it wasn't nurturing me at all, and I came to understand that I was trying to play the part of somebody who had an unusually successful and happy marriage. It was all self-delusion, really.

I hope that the case histories above haven't given the impression that if you have problems in your intimate relationships, all you have to do is see a psychic counsellor and they will immediately be resolved. There is always a lot of pain in letting go of the old, in looking clearly at yourself, and in establishing new and healthier ways of behaviour.

Seeing a psychic counsellor is one possible way to start looking at those problems, but nobody should ever imagine that this means somebody else can solve your difficulties for you. A clairvoyant can't tell you what to do, only let you know what he or she sees—and it's up to you to take it from there. Clairvoyance can only be of help if you actually want to solve your problems—some people would rather carry on living with them and not take charge of their own lives.

Any change always involves tremendous effort and also motivation. The following story has nothing directly to do with relationships, but illustrates a common attitude towards change.

Peter had very high blood pressure and was taking medication to bring it down. The pills he took brought down his hypertension, but also had many adverse side-effects which were unwelcome. He was told by his doctor that if he took more exercise, made a conscious effort to relax and meditate, cut down his calorie intake and stopped drinking, he could bring down his blood pressure without medication.

He considered it, but decided:

It was going to be such a horrendous effort doing all those things, I didn't know whether I wanted to make it. For me, food and drink offered comfort, and I felt that on balance, I would rather carry on taking the pills, even with their known side-effects, than to make this effort. Also, at the end of the day there was no absolute guarantee that my blood pressure would go down.

Although I know I would benefit from a healthier way of life, at the moment I don't feel I have the strength to set those lifestyle changes into motion.

As with physical, so with emotional health. After seeing a psychic counsellor, even after taking responsibility, there is no guarantee whatever that life will go smoothly. In fact, the opposite might happen, as life might throw up even more challenges. As somebody once said, ships are very safe in harbour, but that's not what ships are built for. We are meant to face challenges, to learn and grow. The difference is that, with awareness, events can be seen as challenges, as lessons, not as good or bad. The things that happen happen, that's all. How we see them depends on our interpretation.

But to sum up, if you feel ready to handle what might come up, psychic counselling can help you to see what patterns you have been forming in your life, to realize that everything does conform to a pattern of some kind, to see where you might have been sabotaging yourself and what you can do in future to prevent it.

In a sense, all psychic counsellors can help us to do is to become aware of what, really, we already know, but what we may have hidden and denied from ourselves.

If you feel that your personal relationships have never gone right, that there is some important missing ingredient or that you would like to understand more about the nature of love and attraction, rather than proceeding in a fog, then you may feel a psychic counsellor is the right person to help you. Only you, though, can decide what to do as a result of your new knowledge or insight.

If you take such counselling seriously, you will almost certainly become a different person. But you will become more *yourself*, because you are helping the real you to emerge.

SEVEN

PSYCHIC COUNSELLING IN BUSINESS AND PROFESSIONAL LIFE

Perhaps psychic matters seem very far removed from the hard-headed world of business. After all, few business people dealing with balance sheets, expansion programmes and bank loans are likely to be very interested in communicating with discarnate entities, or want to have serious discussions about whether ghosts or fairies exist—at least during office hours. It would hardly seem a necessary adjunct to productivity. Nor are most of them likely to consult a psychic before they make a take-over bid or decide whether to open up another branch. At first glance, the two worlds could not be more dissimilar—the one concerned with the spiritual realm, with eternal realities, the other very much concerned with the here and now, the material world, short-term gains and profits rather than storing up treasures in heaven.

Most religions and spiritual paths have emphasized poverty, rather than riches, as the way to heaven and eternal peace. The Bible reminds us how difficult it is for rich men to be spiritual at the same time, and how we should concentrate on storing up riches in heaven rather than on earth, where they will inevitably perish.

Certainly, most successful business people consider that they have nothing to do with anything psychic—and that meddling in such things would be a waste of their time. They would look at you in astonishment if you suggested that they might themselves be psychic. But the fact is that most people who manage to be successful in the world of business, commerce and financial dealings *are* psychic, whether or not they realize it. This is because, in order to be successful in business—where the price for failure can be extremely high—people have to be able to employ two supremely psychic qualities: intuition and telepathy.

Their intuition or, as they might term it, vision, tells them what they would like to achieve and gives them an insight as to how they might achieve it. They have first to listen to that voice within and be confident when they are hearing it. Most people who have eventually succeeded wonderfully in the business world have managed to hold onto their vision through all kinds of vicissitudes and setbacks, and eventually emerge triumphant—if, that is, their vision is allied to good business sense and marketing skills. Common sense has to come in as well, however, when considering how to bring the vision into some kind of reality.

Having vision, in this sense, does not necessarily mean that humanity is going to be better off or that the envisaged product or service is going to help people lead better lives. A business vision is not the same as a religious vision and it may have nothing to do with any moral sense. It is basically a matter of having the ability to tap into what the public want, at a time when nobody else is providing quite the right product or service. Bringing a new product into being is quite as creative as any work of painting or literature, and 'having a good head for business' is a combination of intuition, intelligence, self-confidence and forward thinking. It involves assessing what is going to be the next big thing that the public are going to want and then going for it.

Telepathy, basically a branch of intuition which involves knowing what other people are thinking or feeling, comes in when dealing with others, trying to persuade them of the rightness of the product or service, and in trying to read the minds of colleagues, potential buyers and employees. Telepathy is used when business people with a potentially good idea are trying to tap the minds of the public to gauge whether their product is truly wanted.

This was what Henry Ford did when he produced cars—previously within reach only of the very rich—for the masses. He foresaw that, given a chance, most people would love to have their very own transport which would enable them to travel when and where they pleased. How right he was. Once people have owned a car, they will give up many things before letting go of their personal vehicle, the trusty steed which symbolizes freedom.

People all over the world want to travel. Perhaps they always have, but certainly in our century more have travelled greater distances than anybody before them. Almost anything which enables people to travel more—bikes, buses, aeroplanes, cheap holidays—has been a successful idea.

Package holidays came in mainly during the 1960s to enable people who had never set foot out of their own country before—and who were understandably nervous about it—to do it with everything arranged for them. The former airline tycoon Freddie Laker had a vision of loads of people being able to travel to exotic countries very cheaply, the kind of people who previously had only been able to consider a trip to the nearest seaside. It was a vision that he was able to bring into reality and very many thousands of people enjoyed cheap Laker holidays to exotic locations before his company went bust. But the idea of cheap holiday travel continues—most of us long to get away, and even if we may not actually enjoy flying, we like the idea that we can be transported thousands of miles in just a few hours.

Visions are important and necessary—but they can be mistaken, as the following examples show.

The computer genius Clive Sinclair got it wrong when he manufactured the C5s, electric cars which went about 20 miles before needing to be recharged. Although we long to have vehicles which do not need to be filled up with petrol all the time, the C5 was too impractical and had too limited a use to appeal to many people. The idea was good—but on this occasion, Clive Sinclair did not tap accurately enough into the intuitive and telepathic sense which had served him so well in bringing computers within the reach of almost every home.

It's always necessary to tap into people's deep longings to launch a successful product. One of the most successful innovations of this century, at least as far as women are concerned, is internal sanitary protection—the idea for which came from a doctor wanting to make life more comfortable for nurses on night duty. The pill, similarly, helped to liberate women from the fear of pregnancy every time they had sex. Again, it proceeded from thought and vision.

I'm not saying that business ideas are motivated by altruism—they're not. But modern psychic thought tells us that there is nothing inherently wrong with the selfish principle— something has to motivate people and if it's profit, that's not necessarily bad. The only time we can question the profit motive is when the outcome will be to degrade or humiliate, just to gain money. If the outcome is a product or service which makes life considerably easier or more enjoyable for large numbers of people, then the motivation doesn't have to be unselfish.

For example, there was a lot of resistance at first to super-markets and hypermarkets—which were opened with the aim of turning a huge profit. But who now wants to go to half a dozen different shops to buy groceries, meat, stationery and fruit and veg, as our mothers and grandmothers did? There has also been a lot of resistance, at least in the UK, to Sunday opening. But go to any supermarket or shopping centre which is open on a Sunday and you'll find it crammed full. We *want* supermarkets, we *want* shops to be open on Sundays—the one day in the week that a majority are at leisure.

A successful business person has to have a vision of what the public wants in the very immediate future. They have to be able to sense what is dead and gone and what is up and coming. Laura Ashley's genius was to give us a glimpse, at affordable prices, of a vanished and more romantic era than our own. In the hard-edged 1960s, she was producing flowery, frilly frocks with their echoes of pastoral life, shepherdesses, a less frenetic and more harmonious lifestyle, a backward look without all the inconveniences that attended past ages. At a time when synthetic fibres were taking over, Laura Ashley shops reminded us that cool cottons, silks and real fabrics still existed and could be worn. Her vision was a success all over the world. When other people tried to imitate the Laura Ashley style, they did not succeed—because they did not have her vision. Of course, astute business sense was needed to translate that vision into a world-class empire, but without the vision, the business sense would have been of little use.

Look also, at how we took to the Habitat style at about the same time—simple wooden furniture, cotton rugs, basic chairs and sofas, immediate comfort allied to modern production methods. Any successful business venture has to appeal to the deepest instincts and wishes within us—at a particular point in time—otherwise it cannot be foisted onto the public. We will only accept what we really want, and all the advertising and persuasive sales talk in the world won't be enough to persuade us otherwise.

Look how difficult enterprising people have found it to establish timeshare apartments and holidays. There was a vision there, undoubtedly. But not that many people are really enamoured of the idea of spending large sums of money on a two-week share in an apartment they have to visit every year whether they like it or not, somewhere that will never be truly theirs. No wonder timeshare firms have to employ the hardest of hard-sell methods to try and persuade enough people to part with their money.

It's a similar story with double-glazing. Although some people were taken in by early sales talk that double-glazing would add to the value of the house and halve fuel bills, it didn't take long to realize that it actually did neither of these things—that it was, in most cases, a waste of money. Therefore, enormously hard-sell methods had to be employed to try and persuade people there was at least some virtue in spending thousands of pounds on this product. In fact, the only people who need double-glazing are those who live near very busy streets and need to keep the noise out. Double-glazing is another example of a business vision which didn't really provide a product that was deeply wanted.

So vision is vital in business—and in fact, psychic awareness is an asset in every aspect of business life, whether one is talking about new products, expansion or keeping existing personnel happy. We need common sense and rationality, of course—but in order to enjoy our work, in order to get the most out of it, to fulfil our own potential and feel we are being useful and productive, we need to harness the right side, the intuitive side, of our brains as well. We need to make sensible use of clairvoyance and intuition, gifts that we all have to some degree.

Yet, although a minute's thought will enable people to realize that without psychic gifts, businesses can get nowhere, the business world has a reputation for being hard, detached, unemotional and highly masculine. Not many businesses are going to welcome astrologers (although in some companies nowadays astrological charts are drawn up for prospective key personnel), and you can imagine the reaction if a high street bank, for instance, announced that it was fixing up crystal healing and aura reading sessions for its staff. As a journalist, I can see that it would make a good story, but I can't imagine anybody taking it all that seriously. No, in enabling business people to become aware of the psychic dimension, other methods have to be used.

Perhaps the most basic, and most important, psychic skill in business is that of communication. No business is going to get very far without effective communication, and in order to put across ideas and present new concepts, there has to be a deep awareness of what one is doing, how one comes across to other people. If people don't like you, if they find you boring or incomprehensible, they're not going to listen—and valuable opportunities will be lost.

Meribeth Bunch is an American communications consultant currently working in the UK. She works mainly with multinationals and other large firms and leading charities, holding seminars and group and individual sessions on how to use imagination, an awareness of choice and an understanding of others in the business world.

She said:

I wouldn't call myself a psychic counsellor, as that for so many people implies spiritualism, or weird practices. But what I try to do is to show people how they can use their imaginations, go with their gut feelings and use their intuition to get the best out of their business, their colleagues and themselves.

Many people believe that in the business world you have to be hard-nosed and have a sense of detachment. They think that using intuition and imagination is out of place. When I hold seminars or individual sessions, I don't go into a trance or tune in to outside entities. If I did, I wouldn't get the jobs, as people want practical advice.

On the other hand, the advice I give is different from ordinary business advice. I try to get people to understand that even in a strict hierarchical organization, each person brings his or her separate identity to the job and that they are going to remain an individual.

The first thing I do is to sit people down and ask them what they want from their job. Many feel that things could be improved, without knowing what, or how.

People often feel when working in big companies that they get swallowed up, that there is no room for any personal identity. This is where imagination comes in, Meribeth said.

People often believe they have no personal space, that they don't have any choice in their work, or how they present themselves. One of the first things I do is to remind people that they always have options. This is where imagination and vision comes in. Many people working in offices believe they do nothing to create the atmosphere they work in, that it has nothing whatever to do with them.

In fact, we are all creating an atmosphere all the time, and we can, if we like, choose to change or improve it. I'm amazed at how many workers feel that there is nothing whatever they can change, either about themselves or their working environment. I remind them that they can change anything, that they can put themselves in charge.

Those working in a fixed hierarchy often believe they have no choice, but this is never true. Also, when workers believe this, they are doing nothing to help the business. One of my main tenets is discussing with workers how an awareness of choice improves the business environment. It empowers both you and the people around you.

The critical element in business today, said Meribeth, is that there is more responsibility and there are more options than ever before. Nobody nowadays is just a cog in the machine, 'just' a secretary or 'just' a receptionist, but all play their part in creating the ambience of the office, department store or supermarket.

Many people these days speak of work-related stress. Countless studies have pointed out that this is due in large part to a perceived lack of choice in the workplace, to the feeling that one has no choice, but is a passive victim in a big uncaring organization. One of Meribeth's jobs when working in large companies is to try and help employers and employees create a more caring atmosphere, and to remind people that even the biggest and most efficient organization is only made up of individuals. She also reminds all personnel, whether they are in 'key' positions or lower down the ladder, that they always have far more choice than they realize.

Even if you're in prison, she says, you still have choices— choices about how to behave to the warders and to the other inmates, and you can choose whether to have a negative or positive attitude. You can choose to be resentful and bitter or you can view a stretch in prison as an opportunity to learn valuable lessons about human nature in a fearful, inharmonious atmosphere. Meribeth said:

> I use the prison analogy, simply because people often believe when in the workplace that they are serving a kind of prison sentence, that they have few choices and that they are always at the mercy of those above them, those in executive or higher positions.
>
> Even those people in executive positions often believe they must act in certain preconceived ways, that there is nothing they can do to change anything. This leads to despair and stress, because all individuals are happiest when they feel they have at least some control over their environment, their emotions and their attitudes.
>
> A lot of people get into executive positions by copying the person above them, but copying behaviour will only ever set in motion short-term gains. Instead of blindly copying, people can learn to be themselves and also satisfy the needs of the company.
>
> People change when they are ready to change.
>
> I'm not there to tell the company how to run itself, but to show people how they can be more effective communicators—by being themselves and by realizing that they have far more power in the corporate structure than they may have realized.

The essence of Meribeth's seminars, which focus a lot on body language and the unconscious signals we put out and get back, is that we all create an atmosphere around us. Psychics might call this the aura, while a more scientifically-minded person might describe it as a force-field. Whatever, the fact is that every single person in an organization, from the doorman to the tealady, puts out an atmosphere and this subtly affects the whole organization. It's a mistake to think that only the people at the top create an atmosphere.

We can all make our offices friendly or unfriendly, welcoming or unwelcoming, whatever our position, simply by our attitude. We can create a feeling of harmony or disharmony in our own personal space, however cramped that space may be.

Meribeth teaches key personnel how they can make sure they are creating the best possible atmosphere around their personal space by awareness of their body language, their gestures, their posture and the way they speak.

> One young woman who had to give presentations, but felt she wasn't putting over a very strong image, never looked at me the whole time we were talking. Instead, her eyes were closed. This meant that her presence wasn't there, which made it very difficult indeed to listen to her.

When we feel we are in control, when we feel we can direct our emotions and attitudes, that is when the intuitive and telepathic gifts can come into their own. If we can connect with ourselves, we can also connect to other people at work, 'know' what they are thinking and feeling, and act accordingly. It is up to all of us who are in regular work to create the best possible atmosphere, both for our own sake and the sake of the company.

When people realize they have choice, that they don't have to be passive victims, they can then start asking themselves what they really want, and how they might be able to bring this about. Not everybody is going to have the kind of vision which will turn them into a world-class business person, but we can all sharpen up our intuition and awareness to realize that when we employ these gifts, we can also start to fulfil our own potential. I believe that 'standard' psychic counselling, where you have a session with a clairvoyant to gain clarification, can be of enormous help in the business world.

The intuitive approach can also be applied at company level. *Marsha George* is an American management consultant currently working near Bath, and a co-director of the business consultants Maclean and George. She specializes in the intuitive approach and, unlike most other management consultants, looks for the underlying unconscious and emotional attitudes which pervade large companies, and then helps key personnel to bring them to conscious awareness.

She said:

> We get called in usually when businesses are going through a very bad patch and are worried about their survival.
>
> Our job is to help individuals learn more about the way they operate by enabling them to look at the deep-seated unconscious patterns in their work and bring them to the surface. We use the notions known long ago in alchemy, where one metal is transformed into another. We provide the stable container and apply the heat, so that companies can be healthily transformed.
>
> We do this by bringing groups of people together and instituting a dialogue between them. We feel that the right kind of dialogue can transform an organization, so that people start to think differently.

This, says Marsha, suits any company which has got stuck into inappropriate ways of conducting itself.

> For instance, we are called in a lot nowadays by local authorities who are being pushed by central government into delivering a new type of service.
>
> Very often, they don't know how to change themselves, so we help them to get away from purely mechanical solutions by uncovering this emotional layer. Basically, we help companies and organizations to connect with customers and consumers, to empathize with them. As with individuals, no company can be successful until it has got its own internal house in order.
>
> Most management consultants are not working in this intuitive, psychic way, but to my mind it is the only way forward. The time has come when companies and individuals have to look deeply at what they are doing, in order to change habitual patterns to operate in a healthier, more functional way.

An increasing number of firms are now also employing financial astrologers, graphologists and other psychically gifted people to assess job ventures and help with job applications.

Financial astrology has been extensively used for a number of years in Wall Street, where highly specialized cycles are drawn up to assess market trends and financial speculations. As with psychological astrology, the key is synchronicity, seeing the connection between earthly and heavenly events, rather than attributing any direct influence of the planet of monetary affairs.

Graphology is mainly used to assess potential new personnel. If ever you are asked to send a letter of application in your own handwriting, you can be sure that a graphologist will be asked to assess it. In France, almost all large companies use graphologists, and the practice is fast-growing in Britain and America.

Duncan McIntosh has been a professional graphologist for over 30 years and although he does work with individuals, most of his work is now with large companies. He said:

> There has been a long resistance to using graphology, but now that ever more businesses are discovering how successful it is, this method of assessment is growing fast.
>
> In France, 75 per cent of executives get their job through a handwriting test, and to my mind, nothing is more accurate. Once you learn how to read it, handwriting tells you everything you need to know about a person, including their state of health and any major operations they have had.
>
> Just recently, I looked at one woman's handwriting and asked her if she had a long scar on her abdomen. She looked at me in surprise and said yes, she'd had a major stomach operation some years before. It showed up in her handwriting.

Graphology, said Duncan, is both a science and an art, and as with astrology or palmistry, a large amount of intuition is needed for accurate interpretation.

The reason it works so well in the business world is that it tells you whether a particular person is suited to being an accountant, a secretary, a middle manager or can go right to the top.

If the firm wants to appoint a new accountant, I look for signs of concentration and honesty in the handwriting. If the handwriting shows deviousness, I would advise against employing this person, however impressive the CV was.

I would also be looking for organizational abilities, especially if the boss was not a well-organized person.

Very many people, said Duncan, are in the wrong jobs—but a detailed handwriting analysis would prevent this.

At the moment, the British government is handing out money to people to start businesses who haven't a hope in hell of succeeding. Somebody who writes with very light pressure, for instance, would be very modest and not have strong will power. They may be extremely artistic, though, and might be good as keeper of the Queen's pictures, for instance. But they would not succeed in the harsh business world where there is a lot of hassle.

Handwriting which slopes to the left generally indicates an introvert, somebody who does not like or welcome change. An introvert, though, would be able to work in the kind of confined space which would be overwhelmingly claustrophobic to an extrovert.

Writing which leans to the right, is fast and glides easily over the paper indicates a person who will be ready and eager to accept new challenges, new ideas. Very heavy pressure is indicative of somebody with great energy, somebody who probably likes the good things of life, such as food and drink, and who may well be overweight.

Duncan McIntosh believes graphology has been slow in taking its rightful place because so few people are prepared to look inside themselves.

> We have concentrated on the externals, especially in the business world, and that is one reason why things so often go wrong. To my mind, graphology is a technique whose time has come, and it is one of the fastest-growing methods of recruitment analysis.

Whatever type of handwriting we are taught, says Duncan, we soon individualize it, making it our very own. A personal style of handwriting develops in early teenage years and then settles down into a broad style which continues for life. As people get older, their handwriting develops and changes, and in these changes is embodied all their life's experience. This is why it is so difficult to forge handwriting and also why it is almost impossible for people to change their handwriting consciously.

In America, medical graphology is now becoming widely used to diagnose illnesses. Duncan said:

> The handwriting of a well person looks completely different from that of somebody suffering chronic illness. You can diagnose cancer, heart problems and other diseases through handwriting. It's also possible to tell the handwriting of a homosexual and usually it will be clear whether the writer is male or female.
>
> Women's handwriting on the whole is clearer and more aesthetically pleasing than that of men. This is because they tend to be more relaxed and less uptight about their emotions.

Quite apart from recruitment, psychic counselling may also be of use if you have a vision of creating some kind of business. It may be worth checking it out to see whether you really, deeply, have this vision or whether you simply want the adulation, fame and money that you expect will be yours with a good business idea. A practised psychic can, by assessing and interpreting the energies around you, help you to amplify what is in your mind, and bring it to conscious awareness. This can help you to think a possible bright idea through and go with your gut reaction as to whether it's such a good idea after all. You never know—it might be a far better idea than you ever imagined.

Never, ever, discount the psychic factor when considering starting a business, setting up on your own or changing career. Unless this X-factor is present, failure and depression can only result.

One man I know changed his career without regard to his personality or gut feelings—and it was a disaster. He had taken a fine art degree and for many years taught in schools. He enjoyed this work and particularly liked teaching artistically gifted pupils. It was this, he said, which made it all worthwhile. He also liked the camaraderie of the classroom, the long holidays and the fact that, in any large school, there are bound to be at least one or two teachers with whom it's possible to establish a rapport.

But as time went by and he got married and had a family, he began to feel that teaching wasn't paying enough. He decided to train as an accountant so that he could make lots of money. Because he was a very clever person, he managed to pass his exams, although it was a long hard struggle.

But although he eventually qualified as an accountant, because his heart wasn't in it, because he hated the short holidays, the lack of interesting company in offices and being confined to a little office all day long, he was never a success— and never earned as much as an accountant as he had done in teaching.

He is now back teaching, not fine art, but business studies— and loves it, but feels the years spent trying to gain accountancy qualifications were wasted.

Although he went to a careers analyst for advice before embarking on the accountancy course, if, instead, he'd been to a reputable psychic, he might well have been enabled to amplify and bring to conscious awareness what he really wanted. He thought he *ought* to want more money, because he was now married—but in fact, as he now realizes, there are other things, such as stimulating companionship and the time to read books, go to exhibitions and travel, that are far more important.

Very often, people will not consider going to see a psychic, or any other type of advisor, until their lives are acutely uncomfortable. In the business world, few things create greater discomfort than the failure of a venture, or redundancy. Yet, with psychic awareness, these things can be viewed not as a terrible tragedy but as an opportunity to become introspective, to discover one's true self.

One psychic who sees a lot of people who have been made redundant said:

> Usually when people are first made redundant, they panic and wonder what on earth they are going to do, how they are going to manage for money and how on earth they are going to find another job.
>
> But often, as they think about it more and come to terms with it, they start changing their attitude to one of, 'Thank God I was made redundant, now I can do what I've always wanted to do.' Very often, people have to suffer before they learn who they are. Those who are made redundant have to ask themselves important questions, such as, 'Does, or did, this job have anything to do with my status, my personality, my view of myself as a human being?'
>
> It seems to me that the greatest lesson anybody made redundant can learn is that they can emerge intact, even when their job or business has crashed around their ears.
>
> Such people often realize that they can now use their creative side. They often become very successful after redundancy because they are at the edge, and being at the very edge makes them be more creative, call all their resources together and see how they can be utilized.

Whenever apparently bad things happen, the question to ask always is: 'What is the lesson for me here, what do I need to learn from this experience so that I can make the most of it and progress?' We also have to learn that we create our own misery. Obviously we can be hungry and cold, and these are not comfortable states to be in. But we don't have to be miserable.

What psychic awareness teaches us here is that in the world of business, as in any other, universal laws apply. We get back what we give out and we create our own reality, to use a somewhat hackneyed New Age phrase.

So what about money—after all, isn't that what business success is all about? How many of us would go into work every day if we simply didn't need the money? Are psychics the best people to advise us here, especially as we have seen that most do not concern themselves with financial gain?

What psychics can do here is to help you clarify your attitude to money—what you see it as doing for you, why you may feel you don't have enough and what you can do to attract more of it into your life. Then, once you have been able to clarify your attitude towards money, you can be clearer about how you can make it work better for you, take charge of your own finances and not bury your head in the sand about them.

There are now, on both sides of the Atlantic, 'prosperity consultants' working to help people have a better attitude towards money, to replace 'poverty consciousness' by 'prosperity consciousness'. In essence, this means that you *already* regard yourself as being wealthy rather than poor, and inculcate the attitude that money flows to you easily and naturally, and that you will always have enough to meet your needs.

Prosperity consultants who work with psychic awareness remind clients that money is above all, a means of exchange, a transfer of energy. Whenever considering a new purchase, the question must always be asked: 'Would I rather have the money or this item?' If you decide that you would prefer the item, then yield up the money gladly and without resentment, because you have secured the item in its place. There has then been a fair exchange. If you don't feel the exchange is fair, if you don't really want the goods or are aghast at the price, then don't buy them.

You should always remind yourself that you are worth the best—not necessarily always the most expensive, but the item that would best serve your purposes. For instance, if you are a very keen gardener, there is no point in buying cheap tools, but if you dig out and replant a window box twice a year, then the cheapest possible trowel will be all you need.

If you bear in mind that you deserve the best possible product, then you are unlikely to make mistakes or to economize ridiculously because you have overspent ridiculously. You will have chosen *appropriately*.

The concept of prosperity consciousness has nothing to do with winning the pools, nor does it mean you have to think wistfully of all the wonderful things you'd do if a long-lost uncle suddenly left you a fortune. It does not, either, mean that you just sit and wait for the money to come in, without doing anything to bring it in. You have to keep working, keep monitoring what your money is doing, but you do it without anxiety, with a light instead of a heavy heart.

Taking on board this concept also means that you know you that you deserve a good rate for your work, and that you should not undersell yourself or consider you are second-best and not worth what other people doing a similar job are getting. It means that you insist on the proper rate for the job and that you are prepared to take your skills elsewhere if they are not being appreciated at your present place of work. It means that you have the confidence to apply for promotion and to expect to get it.

It does not necessarily mean that you will become super-rich like the Sultan of Brunei, but that you will always have enough to meet your needs. You will not take on huge financial burdens that are going to make life uncomfortable, because you will have an awareness of needing to feel comfortable, in harmony, at peace with your financial situation.

At the same time, an awareness of prosperity consciousness means that you will be prepared to take risks, not always to play safe, but to be able to calculate what is the sensible risk on such and such a purchase, investment or expenditure. It means you will not close your eyes to the consequences of your actions or have the wool pulled over your eyes by smart-talking financial advisors who speak seductively of get-rich-quick schemes. There is no such thing. Money, like everything else in life, obeys universal laws. You are unlikely to get anything for nothing. If you always have the feeling that you are rich, that you have enough—whatever your situation appears like to others—then you will have enough. Some of the new spiritual movements which have sprung up in the twentieth century adhere to the philosophy that there is enough for everybody in the universe—we just have to realize it. And a giving spirit attracts money, while a mean spirit sends it away.

It may seem that all this talk about money and business is not very spiritual—but we ignore it at our peril. In our world today, whether we like it or not, money is the main means of exchange and we live in a society which runs primarily on financial principles.

We must use money sensibly, not for self-aggrandizement, not to impress others, not to make others feel envious and downtrodden, not to parade our wealth or to moan about how poverty-stricken we are and how unfair it all is, but as something potentially beneficent that we can harness for our own good. We must neither squander nor hang on to it, nor think it's clever not to have any sense about money or any interest in it. We must use it like any other source of energy—and realize that, as with psychic gifts themselves, money is neither good nor bad. It is simply a commodity, simply the means by which we exchange goods and services, ours to enjoy and utilize to the best of our ability.

EIGHT

COULD YOU BE PSYCHIC?

People often think it must be wonderful to be psychic, to be able to read others like a book and foretell what is happening. In some ways, of course, it is. But sometimes, this clear sight can be a burden and a problem for those who possess it. It can often be a good thing *not* to see too much, not to know what is going on in people's minds. Would you really want to be bothered by all those discarnate entities on the astral plane trying to bend your ear and get a word in edgeways?

Throughout history, seers, soothsayers and clairvoyants have not had an easy time. As we have seen, it has frequently been their fate not to be believed, even when they knew for an absolute certainty what was going to happen. Greek myths are full of prophecies which cannot be circumvented and the tragedy always is that nobody heeds the warning. Or, if they listen to the oracle, they try not to take any notice of it. Not much has changed today.

Also, if you think about it, it must be very disconcerting to hear voices, to see things which for other people aren't there, to 'know' things which are hidden from others or to be in contact—or imagine you are, which in this case comes to the same thing—with entities or energies from sources denied the majority. If nothing else, it sets you apart from other people and that's not always a comfortable place to be. People gifted with 'second sight' or clairvoyance often find that others regard them as being round the bend, mentally ill or, at the very least, highly peculiar.

But there seems little doubt that people are becoming more psychic than before. We are now starting to acknowledge that small children are probably psychic, as animals are, in that they often 'know' things without knowing how they know them, and it seems that adults are becoming more psychically aware as well.

Of course, we cannot know for sure whether it is that people are actually becoming increasingly psychic or whether as a society, we are starting to accept the validity of this other source of information. Probably a combination of both.

The problem is that, if you are psychic, you are liable to be more open to all kinds of impressions, good and bad. You may feel that your world is absolutely crowded with people, entities and impressions, even at times when you would prefer to be alone. This is why those people who have become dramatically aware of a psychic gift and wish to use it properly, have to learn how to 'shut down' and 'open up' at will, so that the psychic faculty can be harnessed and used for positive purposes. Otherwise, there is no effective filter operating to shut out the undesirable voices or impressions.

In his book *Hungry Ghosts*, Joe Fisher gives examples of psychically gifted people who allow 'bad spirits' to come through them as well as good ones. As we have seen before, the psychic gift is neutral and is just as capable of allowing harm to come through as good.

Although very few people are highly powerful psychics, in the same way that very few are world-class concert pianists or famous artists, most of us have at least a degree of psychic ability. How acute is yours? Answering the following questions will give you some idea as to how psychic you might be naturally:

As a child, did you have an imaginary friend who was very real to you?

Do you sometimes get a strong feeling when a friend or relative is about to phone, write or otherwise get in contact?

Do you often know who is on the telephone before you pick up the receiver?

Do you ever get strong sensations about a particular place or building?

Can you hold a personal object in your hand, such as a ring or necklace, and 'read' the history of the owner from it?

Have you ever had a strong premonition about something which is about to happen, whether for good or ill?

Do there seem to be a lot of coincidences in your life that you cannot easily explain?

Do you ever see auras or halos around people?

Have you ever had the feeling that you have 'gone out', in some sense, of your body?

Have you ever heard voices in your head telling you what to do?

Have you ever quite clearly seen a ghost?

Have you ever had the feeling that somebody or something outside you is directing what you do?

If a writer, painter or musician, do you sometimes get the feeling that an unseen hand is guiding you or that somebody is 'taking over' from you as you create?

Do you ever get the feeling that some things are 'meant'?

Does electrical equipment often go wrong around you?

Have you ever witnessed objects moving of their own accord?

Have you been quite clear in your mind that an event was about to happen and then it happened just as you had seen it?

The more times you said yes, the more psychic you are. Even if you answered yes to only one question, then you are at least slightly psychic.

Ivy Northage, in her book *Mediumship Made Simple*, adds the following. You are undoubtedly psychic, she says, if you dream prophetically, have hunches, see bright lights flashing across a book you are reading, have premonitions and hear voices.

So, if you feel you might be psychic, how should you make the most of your gifts?

Most practising mediums and psychics give very clear advice and also stern warnings about accessing the psychic faculty. It should always be done, they say, with full consciousness and awareness, and an understanding that it must not be used for self-aggrandizement, egotistical purposes or personal advancement. It should never be used for personal fame or fortune, or to try and gain power over others. Misuse of the psychic gifts, they warn darkly, will only bring despair and misery, because 'universal laws' in these matters have to be obeyed. Try to flaunt them and chaos will result. The universal law that operates in relation to psychic gifts states that they should be harnessed only to increase harmony, love and connectedness on the planet. Use them for selfish gain and the rewards will be short-lived and not worth having.

In a little book called *The Psychic Powers and their Development*, published by the College of Psychic Studies in 1974, mediums Helen Macgregor and Margaret Underhill describe how they understand psychic matters. When psychic gifts are first aroused, they say, rather than being allowed to remain in abeyance, they are often accompanied by what appears to be quite severe emotional disturbance. All of a sudden, messages seem to be coming from everywhere and everything appears to be going out of control. The first thing that will happen is that you will become far more open to all kinds of influences and suggestions. These may be beneficial or harmful and there may be at first no way of telling which is which.

Because of this, the psychically gifted must be even more keenly aware than other people not to lose the intellectual or discriminatory side of their nature, and to make sure that what appears to come from another source, from voices in the head or from other paranormal means, is actually something worth hearing. It's easy, say Macgregor and Underhill, to delude yourself that you possess exceptional powers just because of your ability to see visions. But visions and voices can be meaningless unless they point the way to some individual growth.

All mediums warn that there are a lot of mischievous disembodied spirits about, and that when people die, or pass on, they are not suddenly automatically full of wisdom and a wish to serve those humans down on the earthly plane. Those who have studied such matters, largely through regressing people into their past lives, believe that the 'astral plane' is crowded with those who cannot accept that they don't have bodies and are forever trying to interfere in life down here by targeting mediums and trying to speak through them.

Whether or not you feel you can believe this, it is logical to assume that if voices can tell you to do good things, they can instruct you to do harm as well, like Jesus when tempted by Satan in the wilderness or Thomas à Becket trying not to be influenced by the tempting voices he hears in T. S. Eliot's *Murder in the Cathedral*.

Mediumship, say Macgregor and Underhill, has in itself nothing to do with goodness or evil, intelligence or ignorance. It is simply a faculty and is bestowed on individuals without regard to their morals or principles.

For example, the late fraudulent tycoon Robert Maxwell was undoubtedly psychic: it was this quality, really, that enabled him to keep going for so long. He was able to read people's minds, see what they wanted, allay their fears and tell them what they most wanted to hear. Linked to this was a remarkable facility for languages. Over the years, he actually came to believe that he was some kind of miracle worker, somebody for whom everything would always go right. But because he so flagrantly flaunted universal laws, those whose hopes and ambitions he raised were to be cruelly disappointed in him.

One former Maxwell executive told me that he would take prospective employees out to lunch and ask what their salaries were. Knowing how most people feel they are desperately underpaid and would love loads more money, and also understanding how most of us are tainted at least to some degree with greed, he would lean over and say, 'I'll triple it.' Not double it, mind you, but *triple* it. Who could refuse such largesse?

Unfortunately his psychic gift was capricious and out of control. It was never allied to a good character, so no ultimate benefit was ever derived from his undoubtedly unusual powers.

Another twentieth-century figure who possessed remarkable psychic gifts was the osteopath Stephen Ward, who committed suicide when he was accused of being a pimp. Ward, who was a gifted healer, used his psychic gifts to inveigle himself into high society and to try to manipulate those in high places. Again, no good came of it. No good *could* come of it.

Possibly Maxwell and Ward did not consciously realize they were psychic, but they both understood they had unusual powers of persuasion. Their problem was that they started to believe they were above the law, that because they were so special nothing could touch them.

Macgregor and Underhill point out that psychic gifts must never be used to gain advantage over others or to pry into people's lives. 'When you use higher gifts,' they write, 'these are subject to divine principles.' Whenever psychic gifts are used to bring about injurious, illegal or self-aggrandizing results, only harm can result.

Macgregor and Underhill also say that we should be in awe of psychic gifts, because they will affect everything we do. They will change our attitudes and may even change our lives. Once they are accessed and admitted, we may find we can no longer continue in our previous lives or relationships, but have to make radical alterations. It is often awareness of a psychic gift which makes people leave comfortable, easy lifestyles and risk danger and opprobrium from others.

Once Florence Nightingale became aware of her own psychic gifts, for example, she could no longer continue with the lazy, leisured life in which she had been brought up. She could have had money, marriage, parties, social life—except that she listened to her voices. Once she heard them, she could not continue in what to her became an empty, hedonistic way of life. She *had* to go to the Crimea; she *had* to work hard to establish nursing as a proper profession.

All those who have a vision, who want to usher in something better, who are pioneers in their field, are psychically gifted. They can see quite clearly what others can't—and often feel they have no choice but to act on it. Most of us muddle along in a fog, but those with psychic gifts can't. Once psychic powers are admitted, life is seen from an entirely new perspective. Everything takes on a more serious and urgent tone, and there is no longer any place for shallow hedonism, if the gifts are to be used responsibly.

Ivy Northage believes that mediumship should be regarded as a vocation or calling and as such should be treated seriously. Most practising mediums are very, very serious people indeed, individuals who do not take their gift lightly. They feel a weight of responsibility, because they know they have some extra power and can, if they are not very careful, affect people's lives. We are all influenced by those who tell us what we most want to hear. We imagine we are sceptical and rational but, in reality, most of us are extremely gullible and suggestible. How else would be we so easily taken in by TV advertising, by smooth-talking salesmen, by those who promise us wealth, fame and success?

Ivy goes on to say that the first thing that people find, when they have accepted the reality of the psychic realm, is that they become calmer and more peaceful than before. As they are now tapping into a different dimension, they know that earthly things are impermanent, that what seems horrific today may be a blessing tomorrow and vice versa. Such people learn to look at everything with a sense of calm detachment. This does not mean that they don't enter fully into life on earth, but that they become strong enough not to be swayed this way and that by strong emotions, either their own or other people's. There is increased self-confidence and self-esteem, and a sense of peace which cannot be diminished by events. Gradually, negative emotions and attitudes are replaced by positive ones. Greed, envy, anger and hate disappear, to be replaced by a feeling of love and positivity.

In his book *Looking into the Invisible*, Omraan Mikhael Aivanhov says that when trying to cultivate powers of clairvoyance, it is essential first to be able to control lusts and 'baser instincts', otherwise these will emerge in technicolour, as they did with Robert Maxwell and Stephen Ward. In order to use clairvoyant gifts responsibly, people have first to develop the gifts of love, kindness and inner strength.

The late medium Ena Twigg used to say in her talks that anybody who wanted to increase their psychic gifts should get into the habit of sending out loving thoughts all the time and most particularly when they passed by dark and dismal places such as prisons or hospitals. She believed that sending out these vibrations could only help, whereas if we shuddered and felt horror, we were only adding to the immense amount of negativity and fear already present in these places.

Becoming a medium, says Ivy Northage, means to surrender yourself to the spirit world to become a bridge between the earthly and the ethereal planes in order to help those who need it.

Practising mediums point out that there should also be an alliance between the higher mind, where psychic faculties originate, and the intellect. Mediumistic powers can never be seen as a substitute for intellectual rigour, but both must act together if any genuine creative work is to be achieved.

All practising psychics emphasize that the most important aspect of harnessing clairvoyant gifts is to accept the spiritual dimension of life and to realize that you are receiving vibrations on a level beyond the realm of physical matter. Whatever sceptics may say, these transcendental realms are a definite reality to those who have highly developed psychic gifts.

For those who are concerned to try and *prove* that the spirit world is a reality, Ivy says that scientific explanations for psychic or paranormal events are unlikely to be satisfactory. Of course, this doesn't prove that such events don't exist. There are many things impossible to prove in double-blind clinical trials. Whoever has managed to set up laboratory experiments which prove there are such emotions as joy and bliss, for example? But we all know they exist—in fact *feelings* are the ultimate reality.

The problem with the paranormal world is that not everybody has had direct experience of it—and so trying to persuade people of its reality is problematic.

Perhaps instead of trying to prove it, we should just look at the outcome and ask ourselves whether those who possess psychic gifts seem to be different from others. I think we would have to answer that, yes, they do.

The whole object of mediumship is, or should be, says Ivy Northage, to open up the higher faculties to become more sensitive, more in tune with others, more in tune with oneself. Possession of highly developed psychic gifts means that every experience will be heightened and more intensive than for those who possess only rudimentary psychic awareness.

Aivanhov warns, however, that we should not be in a hurry to become clairvoyant and adds that many clairvoyants are 'wretched people'. Another warning he gives is that if you feel you are clairvoyant, keep quiet about it unless you intend to become a professional psychic, otherwise you will be besieged with questions such as 'Whom will I marry?' 'Will I be rich?' 'Will I be successful?' 'What will become of *you* in all this?' he asks. It's easy to become dragged down by other people once a psychic gift is made public.

In his book *How to Develop your ESP*, Zak Martin points out that everything in the universe operates by a kind of ESP, in that it all happens at a level below the conscious. The ability of a rubber band to stretch back to its original state is, he says, an act of memory which is a kind of extra-sensory perception. Ants use ESP to enable them to get back to their nests, often over distances of many miles.

Most of us, he says, are protected from receiving too many psychic impressions and it may be better that way. If we were picking up psychic impressions all the time the mind could not cope and would become overloaded, a jumble. Mnemonists, those who can never forget anything, people for whom impressions remain as vivid as when first experienced, are known in psychiatry for being very sad cases indeed. Our 'forgetting' is as a safety valve, a device which works for our own protection.

But there is nothing wrong with developing our ESP to a level where we can become more self-aware, and learn to harness the values of peace, love and co-operation, rather than those of aggression, hatred and fierce competition, all of which separate us from other people and instil fear.

Those who are serious about developing their ESP have first to understand the value of meditation and relaxation. Conscious concentration, says Zak Martin, is stressful and produces tension. Great insights come when the mind is clear and clarity of thought is possible only in deep solitude. Most, if not all, great creative works have come out of solitude and there must be a willingness to become introspective. Very many people who never believed they had any psychic gifts at all have discovered them by being able to meditate.

On the practical side, the usual advice for those wishing to develop and increase their powers of ESP is to keep a 'prediction diary'. Write down the name of the next person who you imagine will ring you and then see if you are right. Keep doing this and soon you will find that you are making accurate guesses.

Of course, with all such matters, it's important to distinguish between genuine ESP and wishful thinking. I may long and long and long for a particular person to ring, but this longing will have no effect whatever. Indeed, it could even make the person less likely to ring. What you have to do is to consider who is likely to ring you, rather than the person you would most like to contact you in this way. Don't be afraid to make mistakes, as even the most powerful mediums don't get it right all the time.

The way to increase such powers, says Zak Martin, is to behave as though such information were already known to you, but you have forgotten it. In fact, many people gifted with psychic powers have the strong feeling that they are trying to bring to a conscious level information they actually already know.

When the Egyptologist Omm Sety—Dorothy Eady—was about four years old, she was taken to the British Museum in London. Her parents expected her to be bored stiff, but found that instead she ran with delight to the Egyptian room and stayed there for hours and hours, reading the hieroglyphics.

When the adults told her she couldn't possibly understand what they said, she replied, 'Yes, I do, but I've just forgotten.'

Many professional psychics have the strong feeling when they are holding consultations that they are simply trying to remember, to call to conscious awareness what they already know.

I often feel when I meet somebody new with whom I have a strong rapport that I already know them very well, and that every time I meet them, I am just remembering what, at some level, I already know. As more is revealed, nothing seems to be a surprise, but just fits in to complete the jigsaw.

Feelings can be very accurate in our relationships with other people. If I meet a person for whom I get the very strong feeling, then this meeting is significant. I'm not just talking here about emotional or intimate attachments, but people who may be important to me in my career or other ways unconnected with a love attachment. There have been many times when I have met people whom I would like to be significant in my life, on an intellectual or reasoning level, but it just hasn't happened. You either click instantly or not at all. The trick is to trust this instant rapport and not try to force it when it isn't there.

In establishing psychic links with people, it's always easier with those you know well and for whom there is emotional attachment, than with strangers. So for anybody serious about developing psychic awareness, it's best to start with those closest to you, rather than trying to make such links with complete strangers. One of the differences between ordinary people who may get psychic flashes and professional clairvoyants is that the latter are able to pick up impressions of people with whom they do not have an emotional link. Or perhaps they do make emotional links with strangers, as they do not see them as strangers, but already as brothers and sisters, part of humanity, and thus connected.

Whenever you want to try and make psychic contact, try to establish an emotional link by thinking of the person with love, respect and regard. This will bring them closer to you. Also, you can get into the habit, as Ena Twigg said, of sending out loving thoughts to those in distress or pain. At some level, she believed, people will pick them up and be cheered by them.

I always make a point of sending out loving thoughts to those who are emotionally close to me, but who may be geographically far away or undergoing some important challenge. I used to send out loving thoughts and vibrations to my sons when they were taking important exams. I don't know whether the thoughts made any difference, but they just calmed everything down at a time of potential great stress. I didn't send out 'Pass this exam, pass this exam whatever you do' but 'I wish you well, I'm thinking of you.'

I also send out thoughts to my nearest and dearest when they are about to board a plane, going for a tough interview or having an operation in hospital. Unfortunately, at the moment I can do this only for people who are dear to me, not to those for whom I have no emotional attachment at all. I feel, though, that sending out loving thoughts establishes a bond and enables me to maintain links with them at a time when they may need extra help, even if they are not aware of the source. At the very least, it doesn't do me any harm and it doesn't do them any harm, although it might not protect them from all dangers.

When trying to establish links, it may help to have a photograph of the person or an example of their handwriting. Myself, I feel that handwriting is more personal than a photo and I would rather look at this when thinking of them. I like having photos as well, though, as they also convey some important essence of the person in your thoughts.

This keeping people in your thoughts is not the same as wishing to have power over them, to make them fall in love with you or be in thrall to you. Just the opposite, in fact—it sets them free.

There is also a great difference between keeping people in your thoughts and worrying about them. If you worry about people when they are away or keep telling them that you miss them, you are putting an extra burden on them and making them concerned that they should cause you pain.

When thinking of people who are far away, imagine them having a good time, recovering well or being successful. This removes attention away from you and your worries, and onto positive thoughts about them. Only ever send out good, positive thoughts to others, not curses and ill wishes. These may or may not do the other person harm but they certainly won't do you any good.

Something else you can practise is linking up with everything—animals, flowers and plants as well as people—wishing all creation well, feeling you are a part of it, not separate from it.

Also, if you get premonitions, write these down and monitor them to see how often they come true. Some people imagine that premonitions happen only at times of terrible danger or disaster, but they can happen for good things as well. If you get a 'feeling' that something is about to happen, don't just dismiss it, but go with it.

The more you make ESP part of your everyday life, the more that you come to acknowledge that important information can be revealed to you from sources other than sensory organs, the more powerful your perceptions will become and the more this faculty will work for you.

Sometimes, people who are serious about harnessing psychic abilities become professional clairvoyants themselves. But not everybody has the kind of personality that can cope with lots of people coming with their problems, wanting enlightenment, guidance and clarity in their lives. You have really to be able to wish everybody well—and that's not always easy.

Yet, at the very least, once you take on board the possibility that you too may have psychic abilities, the world will become a much more exciting place. You will take in impressions you previously missed, you will become far more observant, and you will be able to gain instant insights about people and events that may have eluded you before. You will come to know when it is right to set in motion a relationship, to move house, to change jobs or career direction, because you will be obeying your own dictates rather than those set down for you by other people who may know and understand nothing about you, or who may be simply foisting their own wishes onto you. As a simple rule of thumb, if something feels right, go with it. If it doesn't, don't—and wait for more information to be revealed. You will usually know, somewhere inside yourself.

When a psychic's prediction comes true, it can send a shiver down the spine. I once had a psychic reading which foretold two things which did not seem likely to happen at all, let alone in the near future. I could not see, with my reason, how they could possibly come about. Yet within months, both had happened—without my doing anything whatever to bring them about. Once I realized this, I felt quite frightened, as if I had been tapping into dark sources, meddling like Faust with powerful forces. The reason I felt nervous was because of a new awareness that information received by psychic means is at least as important as that we read in the newspapers or see on the television. After the initial nervousness, though, there was a feeling of clarity, of confidence and of certainty that the intuitive or psychic faculty was a clear reality.

The psychic who gave me this information had only—I say 'only', but of course I don't mean it disparagingly—tapped into the energies surrounding me and given back what I was paranormally telling him. In some part of my being, I obviously 'knew' that these events would take place and the shiver was one of recognition: *I already knew!* It made me realize that I, too, had greater powers than I had previously realized. We all have.

I shall probably never have outstanding psychic gifts—if I had, I'm sure they would have become manifest by now—but I know that trusting the intuitive faculty will stand me in good stead, and enable me to have confidence and conviction where previously there would have been fears and doubts. It is there to guide me and to help me tune into myself and others.

In the past, I didn't really know how to say no—and often landed myself in situations which would have been better avoided. Now, when something is presented, I ask myself, 'Do I really want to do this? Does it feel right?' If it does, then I go for it, however bizarre it might seem at the time. If not, then I don't, even if logically it seems the best thing. Our intuitive faculty can see farther than our rational sense, which can only see things in the short term.

The Muse said, 'Look into your heart and write.' If we also learn to look into our hearts and act, we will be developing the psychic faculty in a way that will serve us well and act as a subtle antenna to warn us, guide us and reveal to us what it is right for us to do. It will enable us to have the courage to follow our own path, rather than meekly following those laid down by others, simply because we are too afraid to do anything else.

In benefiting us, a responsible use of the psychic faculty will benefit all we come into contact with as well. We can all become, in a sense, our own psychic counsellors.

SELECTED
BIBLIOGRAPHY

Aivanhov, Omraan Mikhael, *Looking into the Invisible: Intuition, Clairvoyance, Dreams* (Editions Prosveta, 1989).

Campbell, Eileen and Brennan, J. H., *Dictionary of Mind, Body and Spirit* (The Aquarian Press, 1994).

Considine, Mike (ed.), *The Whole Person Catalogue: The Ultimate Source Book for the New Age Seeker* (Brainwave, 1992).

Davies, Rodney, *Discover your Psychic Powers: How to awaken and use extra-sensory perception* (The Aquarian Press, 1992).

Drury, Nevill, *The Visionary Human* (Element Books, 1991).

Ellison, Arthur, *The Reality of the Paranormal* (Harrap, 1989).

Hodgkinson, Liz, *Counselling* (Simon and Schuster, 1992).

--, *Reincarnation: The Evidence* (Piatkus, 1989).

--, *The Personal Growth Handbook* (Piatkus, 1993).

Holbeche, Soozi, *The Power of Gems and Crystals: How they can transform your life* (Piatkus, 1989).

Inglis, Brian, *The Unknown Guest* (Chatto and Windus, 1987).

King, Francis X., *The Encyclopedia of Mind, Magic and Mysteries* (Dorling Kindersley, 1991).

Martin, Zak, *How to Develop your ESP* (The Aquarian Press, 1986).

Northage, Ivy, *Mediumship Made Simple* (Psychic Press, 1986).

Ostrom, Joseph, *Understanding Auras* (The Aquarian Press, 1986).

Petrie, Ann, *Your Psychic World A–Z* (Arrow, 1984).

Reed, Graham, *The Psychology of Anomalous Experience* (Hutchinson, 1972).

Shine, Betty, *Mind Magic* (Bantam, 1991).

Stevenson, Ian, MD, *Children Who Remember Previous Lives: A question of reincarnation* (University Press of Virginia, 1987).

West, D. J., *Psychical Research Today* (Penguin, 1954).

RESOURCES

United Kingdom

The College of Psychic Studies
16 Queensbury Place
London SW7 2EB

Tel: 071-589 3292

Holds courses in psychic unfoldment, lectures, and can also arrange one-to-one sessions with sensitives and mediums affiliated to the College.

Alternatives
St James's Church
197 Piccadilly
London W1V 9LF

Tel: 071-287 6711 and 071-734 4511

Lectures, seminars and workshops on psychic matters are held regularly.

Festival of Mind, Body and Spirit
Arnica House
170 Campden Hill Road
London W8

Tel: 071-938 3788

Holds several healing and psychic festivals a year, where talks and seminars are given by psychic counsellors and healers.

Morning Light
Dalcroy Farm
Tummel Bridge
Nr Pitlochry
Perth
Scotland
PH16 5NT

Tel: 0882 634 230

This residential centre offers counselling and past-life therapy.

Mysteries
9 Monmouth Street
London WC2H 9DA

Tel: 071-240 3688

This bookshop, crammed full of psychic artefacts, can also put you in touch with tarot and palm readers and other psychic counsellors.

Spiritualist Association of Great Britain
33 Belgrave Square
London SW1X 8QL

Tel: 071-235 3351

Very many psychic counsellors, mediums and healers are available for private consultations. All must have shown evidence of psychic gifts before they are allowed to hold sessions at this long-established venue.

Dr Francesca Rossetti
Flat 5
41 Lansdowne Road
London W11

Psycho-Regression Counselling for people suffering from sexual and relationship problems. Also past-life therapy.

The Society for Psychical Research
49 Marloes Road
London W8

Tel: 071-937 8984

This society, founded in 1882, hold lectures, seminars and workshop for those wishing to explore the paranormal in a spirit of scientific investigation. Does not offer psychic counselling.

Psychic News
2 Tavistock Chambers
London WC1

Tel: 071-405 3340

This weekly newspaper, founded in the 1930s, carries many advertisements for psychic counsellors.

Soul-Directed Therapy

Tel: 081-643 4255

Psychiatrist Dr Lisa Sand works with medium Inga Hooper to help clients release past pain (including that accumulated during past lives) quickly and positively.

United States

Common Boundary Inc
7005 Florida St
Chevy Chase, MD 20815

Tel: 301 652 9495

Information on spiritual healing.

New Sense
PO Box 42211
Los Angeles, CA 90042

This newsletter is full of the latest developments in psychology, holistic medicine, meditation, healing, new science and other related topics.

Tarot Network News
271 20th Avenue
San Francisco, CA 94121

This newsletter contains many resources and addresses of people working with the tarot all over the world.

INDEX